The Gringo Guide To Moving To Mexico

Everything You Need To Know Before Moving To Mexico.

Raúl Jiménez

Table of Contents

Introduction

For quite some time, Mexico has been one of the most popular destination countries for those looking to move abroad. Whether you are looking for a place to settle temporarily as you experience a different culture and a relaxed lifestyle, a retirement destination, or you want to become a permanent resident of a foreign country, Mexico is a great option for you. The country is geographically diverse, with lakes, mountains, jungles, remarkable beaches, incredible landscapes, lively, modern cities, and numerous vacation hotspots. This means that there is something for everyone in Mexico. Whether you want to live a modern lifestyle, a laid-back traditional lifestyle, or fast-paced, adventurous lifestyle, you will get it all in Mexico.

Mexico is particularly popular with people from the United States because it is just right next door. Many Americans and Canadians also love Mexico because your dollars will take you way longer in one of the Mexican cities than they would have done in Miami or Ottawa. In addition, there is a huge number of English-speaking people in most Mexican cities, so you can get by even if you know very little Spanish. No wonder the country has become so popular with expats. At the moment, there are close to two million US expats living all over Mexico.

What's more, the country is one of the strongest economies in Latin America. Mexico also shares strong trading ties with the United States, and with many of its cities growing at an impressive rate, it is the perfect destination for someone who is looking for a foreign country to invest in.

If you are already considering moving to Mexico, it is inevitable that you have already heard so much about Mexico. Whether it is about the culture, the food, the cost of living, state of security (or insecurity) within the country, people–even those who haven't been to Mexico–always have so much to say about life in here, and honestly, a lot of it is not even true.

If you are considering moving to the country, it is best for you to be aware of everything you need to know before moving, and who better to tell you what you need to know that someone who has spent his entire life here, and who has helped quite a number of foreigners settle in the country of the Mariachis?

My name is Raúl Jiménez, a 30-year-old author from the state of Tamaulipas in Mexico. I have been tutoring Spanish online for over 3 years on a website known as Italki.com, and so far, I have taught Spanish to almost 200 students from all over the world, including Gabriel Wyner, the writer and founder of Fluent Forever. I have also written an Amazon bestseller on Mexican slang "Mexislang," because I noticed that a lot of Gringos were interested in understanding the language used by locals and understanding how the Mexican mind works. Oh, and in case you are wondering, the word Gringo is the term that local Mexicans used to refer to white people. The term is non-derogatory, so don't mind it when locals use to refer to you as a Gringo.

Over the years, I have guided a number of foreigners, mostly students, and my online friends, around my Small Mexican town, and so I have the experience with the culture shock most of them experience and help them get through with. I even helped one of them get married to a local girl from my own town. Therefore, I have written this book with a good understanding of what gringos go through when they first move to Mexico.

In this book, I am going to tell you everything you need to know about moving to Mexico, including why Mexico is the right choice for you, the immigration process and documentation you need to settle in the country, the cost of living in the country, how to get a grasp of Mexican money, which places you should consider settling in, whether to rent or buy property, all you need to know about crime and narcos, how to handle things like transportation, education for your kids, and health, how to get a job and make a living in Mexico, how to deal with the culture shock and so on.

Excited about the possibility of moving to Mexico? Let's jump right in.

Chapter One: Taking The Decision To Go. Why Mexico?

Located between the US to the north and Belize and Guatemala to the south, a lot of people consider Mexico to be a Pacific Paradise, and it is no wonder it has become one of the most popular expat destinations. But what exactly attracts so many people to Mexico? If you are planning to move and settle abroad, why should you consider Mexico? What are the general advantages of living in Mexico? Mexico has become a top expat destination of choice for a number of reasons, which include:

Friendly Locals

In a number of countries, people are so busy that they have no time for others. Everyone is always rushing somewhere and even getting someone to help you when you are stranded on the street might need a bit of luck. In Mexico, it is the complete opposite. The locals are so nice and kind. Whether you are a tourist or a local, most people will be ready and willing to welcome you with open arms. On the street, people will take their time to say hello, and if you happen to be lost or stranded, many will volunteer to help you, despite the fact that you are a stranger.

Being in the country almost feels like you travelled back in time to a time when people were friendly and courteous and cared about everyone else. Unlike other countries where people believe that time is money and won't spend a few minutes interacting with a stranger or helping them, Mexicans believe that human connections are the most important thing. They believe that a man's character is defined by how he treats other people. It is no wonder that Mexico was ranked as the second happiest country on the planet in 2016's Happy Planet Index.

Therefore, if you are thinking of moving to Mexico, you can expect to interact with a lot of friendly locals, and it won't be a surprise if their happiness rubs off on you.

Getting Residence In Mexico Or Living There Without One Is Easy

Like I mentioned earlier, there are close to 2 million expats from the United States living all over Mexico. When you include expats from other countries, this number balloons significantly. One of the main reasons why there are so many foreigners living in Mexico is that getting residence in the country is quite easy. And the best part? You can live in the country, even if you haven't acquired a residence permit. Yes, that's how welcoming Mexico is.

To get into the country, all you need is your passport. With the passport, you will be issued with a tourist visa which will be given to you either at the Airport or at your point of entry into the country, if you come via land or sea. With this tourist card, you can live in the country for up to six months. Once the tourist visa nears its expiration, you just need to travel outside the country for over 72 hours (usually referred to as a border run) and you will be issued with a fresh tourist visa, allowing you to stay in the country for another six months. Some people live in Mexico this way for years, only making border runs every six months to renew their tourist visa.

The above option is great for those who live part-time in Mexico and part-time in their home country. If you want to settle in the country on a more permanent basis, you should get either the temporary residency visa or permanent residency visa, both of which are quite easy to acquire. Unlike most other countries, Mexico does not have stringent laws that make it difficult to move and settle there. I will take a more detailed look into the documentation you need to settle in Mexico in the next chapter.

Lower Cost Of Living

Another major reason why a lot of people who want to move abroad move to Mexico is that the cost of living in Mexico is significantly lower. You can survive in Mexico with a lot less than you would need to survive in the United States, Canada, The United Kingdom, Sweden, and several other countries. This is especially true when you are not earning your money in Mexico. For instance, if you are an online entrepreneur earning your money in dollars and spending it in pesos, life will become a lot cheaper for you. The prices of most things are much lower in Mexico (real estate, groceries, eating out, labor and services, getting around, and so on). This means that by moving to Mexico, you can significantly lower your living costs while simultaneously increasing your quality of life.

Mexico Is A Modern Country

If you are simply looking for a country that has a lower cost of living, your options are almost endless. There are lots of countries in South America, Africa, and Asia that have a significantly low cost of living. However, what makes Mexico a better choice than most of those other options is that Mexico is a fairly modern country, which means you will reduce your living costs while still getting to enjoy the modern amenities you are used to. You might not have this privilege in some of the other countries.

In Mexico, there are multiple international airports, a well-maintained highway network, cable TV, high-speed internet, including fiber-optic, a widespread and reliable cell-phone network that supports 3G, 4G, and LTE, world-class medical care, huge shopping malls with some popular American chain stores such as Costco and Walmart, gourmet restaurants, and so on. In other words, you will miss none of the modern amenities you are used to. In addition, Mexico enjoys a stable democracy, with a government that functions almost similar to the US government. All these make Mexico a good option for those who want to move abroad but with an experience that is not too foreign.

Climate

Another great thing about Mexico is that you get to enjoy a climate where temperatures are constant all year round. This means that you don't have to worry about snowy winters or extremely hot summers. At the same time, Mexico is a vast country with three different climate zones, so you have the option of choosing a place with a climate that is most suitable to you. If you want to enjoy a temperate climate all year round, you can settle within the central highlands. If you prefer a warmer, more humid climate, you have plenty of choices along the ocean, and the best part is that coastal properties are way more affordable in Mexico compared to the United States. If you want to enjoy cooler temperatures all year round, you can settle in one of the highland mountain times. Whatever kind of climate you prefer, you will find a suitable place in Mexico.

There Are Lots Of Fun Activities In Mexico

Of course, when moving to a foreign country, you want to move to a country that has lots of fun things to do. What's the point of moving to a cheaper country if you cannot even enjoy the money you are saving? Fortunately, there are lots of things to do in Mexico. Most people coming to Mexico are excited about its beaches, and therefore it's no wonder that some of the most popular cities in Mexico are coastal cities like Puerto Vallarta, Cancun, and Cabo San Lucas. However, there is more to Mexico than the beaches. You can wander inland to enjoy the mountains, jungles and other natural wonders within the country, visit smaller towns to experience the Mexican culture, or visit some grand colonial cities like Campeche, Merida and San Miguel de Allende (several have been designated as a UNESCO World Heritage Sites) and enjoy the ancient architecture. There are numerous activities to enjoy in Mexico.

Mexican Food

It is almost impossible to talk about Mexico without speaking about Mexican food. Already, most people in the United States know how tasty Mexican cuisine is. However, when you experience Mexican cuisine locally, in its most authentic form, you will find it to be even more delicious. In the evenings, corner taco stands will open up on the streets of most Mexican towns, where you can enjoy delicacies such as tacos al pastor, a tasty treat that tastes like a blend of Lebanese *Shawarma* kebab and traditional taco. On the Yucatan, you can enjoy delicacies such as *cochinita Pibil*, a tasty pork dish with Mayan influences. In the Southern areas of the country, such as Oaxaca, you will be blown away by the rich mole sauce, while you will find a huge variety of sea-food influenced cuisines in the coastal regions of the country.

Mexican food is a whole attraction by itself, and I will discuss it in greater detail in chapter 12. The best part about enjoying Mexican culinary delights in Mexico is that they are very affordable and fresh. Imagine eating all your favorite Mexican food at half the price you pay for them in the United States or your home country.

Many Mexicans Speak English

Unless you know the native language, moving to a country where English is not spoken can be a very challenging experience. Even simple things like requesting a cab become a nightmare. Fortunately, you don't have to worry about this in Mexico, since a huge number of Mexicans can communicate effectively in English. Therefore, you are unlikely to face any major challenges when doing important things such as processing your residency at the immigration process, ordering food in hotels, conversing with shopkeepers, taxi drivers, and domestic service providers, and so on. However, keep in mind that you will only find many English speakers in the big cities and tourist resort towns. If you plan on venturing to smaller towns and rural areas, however, you will need to know some Spanish, since most people in the rural areas and small towns do not speak English.

A Relaxed Lifestyle

Unlike most people in American cities, Mexicans are not constantly in a hurry. They live life at a much slower pace and are more focused on enjoying life rather than working around the clock. Once you move to Mexico, you will eventually adapt to the relaxed lifestyle and start enjoying every aspect of your life.

Mexico Is Great For Singles

If you are a single person looking to settle abroad, Mexico is a great option for you too. Like I mentioned, Mexicans are friendly and do not shy away from getting into relationships with foreigners, both short term flings and long-term relationships. What's more, unlike in some other countries where locals get into relationships with foreigners either for the money or for a chance to get a foreign visa, most Mexicans get into relationships out of love. In addition, there are some nice resorts and hotels for singles, where you can easily meet someone. Locals also don't have a problem with getting married to foreigners, therefore, if you are a single person looking to settle in Mexico, who knows, you might even end up getting married to a local. Like I mentioned earlier, I even hooked up one of my gringo friends to a local girl from my hometown and they ended up getting married.

Mexico Is Quite Safe

If you ask most gringos who have not set foot in Mexico, a majority of them will tell you that Mexico is a very unsafe place. This perception of Mexico comes from the movies and negative press coverage of Mexico by mainstream media, which is the only source of information a lot of people have about Mexico. However, this view that Mexico is a very dangerous place is not accurate. Most cities within Mexico are pretty safe. Some expats living in Mexico even claim that they feel safer in Mexico than they do in their home countries.

This does not mean that there is no crime and violence in Mexico. The areas near the Northeastern border and areas around Sinaloa, where most of the drug cartels operate from, have very high crime rates, and it is best to avoid them. However, aside from these areas, most of the country is relatively safe. Of course, this does not mean that you should be careless about your safety. For instance, you should be careful when walking at night, whether you are in Guadalajara, New York, or Paris. Don't unnecessarily flash your cash, expensive jewelry, or gadgets. You need to be as vigilant as you would be in any other city. I am going to discuss the issue of safety, crime, and the drug cartels in greater detail in chapter 7.

Mexico Has A Rich Culture And History

Another reason why a lot of gringos love Mexico is the fact that the country has a rich culture and history. Most of Mexico is a blend of the modern and the traditional. While the country and its people are rapidly embracing modernity, they are also not quick to let go of their past. As a result, moving to Mexico allows you to get an experience of ancient Mexican culture and history, without losing access to the modernity that you have become so accustomed to. It is not uncommon to find a parade or procession to celebrate some ancient religious celebration in a Mexican city passing right outside a modern hip art gallery.

Healthcare Is Affordable In Mexico

Like most other things, healthcare is relatively cheap in Mexico. Unless you have a serious illness, you can even survive without the need for medical insurance, although it is always a good idea to have the insurance cover in case you happen to find yourself in a health situation that needs a lot of money. Routine visits to the doctor will cost you less than $50 in Mexico, something you would have paid hundreds of dollars for in the United States. Medications are also relatively cheap. The best part is that you get such affordable healthcare without compromising on the quality of healthcare. In the areas preferred by expats, most of the doctors speak English. You might even come across a number of them who received their medical training in the United States. With such affordable healthcare, it is no wonder that there is an emerging and rapidly growing industry of long term healthcare in residential homes within the country, with costs being up to 10% of what you would expect to pay in the United States.

You Can Practice Your Spanish

If you have always wanted to learn Spanish, what better way to learn the language that by moving to a place that gives you an opportunity to practice the language? Of course, you could also move to Spain, but then everyone speaks Spanish there and very little English, therefore you are going to have quite a hard time expressing yourself before you completely learn the language. In Mexico, on the other hand, a lot of people understand English as well, so you can intersperse English and Spanish as you learn. For instance, when chatting with a waiter or grocery store clerk, greet them in Spanish and speak to them in the little Spanish you know. They will also reply in Spanish, and in case you don't understand, they will explain it in English. This is a fun way to learn a language, and within a few months, you will be able to effectively communicate in Spanish.

Mexico Is Pretty Close To Home

Well, this mostly applies to Americans and Canadians, but it is another reason that makes Mexico a great destination for those seeking to settle abroad. Owing to its proximity to the US and Canada, moving to Mexico is quite easy. Actually, for those in the United States, it is as easy as loading up your stuff into your truck and driving towards the Southern border, with virtually no expenses except for gasoline and toll payments.

The proximity of Mexico to the US and Canada also makes it very easy to visit friends and family back at home. You can get a cheap direct flight from most Mexican cities to your city back at home. Some will even cost you less than $100. Compare this to moving to places such as Asia, where you might need to pay over $1000 to be able to visit home.

Chapter Two: Immigration And Documentation When Moving To Mexico

Since you are planning to settle in Mexico for an extended period, or probably even permanently, you need to be aware of all the documents and requirements you need to live in the country and to understand the country's immigration laws. Fortunately, most of the paperwork you need in order to settle in Mexico can be filled without a lot of hassles. You can easily do it without having to seek the help of an immigration lawyer.

To visit or settle in Mexico, you will typically need one of the following three types of visa or permit:

The Tourist Visa

Also known as the *"Visitante"* permit, this is a permit that is issued to people visiting the country for a short period – mostly tourists and people visiting the country to conduct short-term, non-remunerated business.

In order to receive the Tourist Visa, nationals from the United States, Canada, and most of the countries in Latin America and Western Europe only need to have a valid passport. The tourist visa is usually issued to people from these countries (known as visa-exempt countries) either onboard the flight or at the airport. The cost of getting a tourist visa is usually included in the price of the airline ticket. For those arriving into the country by sea or overland, the tourist will be issued at the point of entry.

If you are from a country that is not classified as visa-exempt, you will need to apply for a tourist visa prior to your visit. In this case, you should consult the website of a Mexican diplomatic body that is closest to you and find out what you will require in order to receive the visa since the requirements for being granted the visa will vary based on the nature of your visit. For people from countries that are not visa-exempt, you will need to pay a tourist visa fee, which currently stands at $36. Your visa will be ready in about two days. Once you receive the tourist visa, it must be used within 90 days. To check whether your country is visa-exempt or not, follow the following link: https://www.visatraveler.com/visa-guides/mexico-visa-requirements/

The tourist visa allows foreigners to stay in Mexico for up to six months (180 days). Once the 180 days are over, you will need to leave the country and come back again in order to receive a fresh tourist visa. This visa cannot be renewed while you are still in Mexico, regardless of whether you come from a visa-exempt country or not.

Foreigners (both from visa-exempt and non-visa-exempt countries) who want to stay in the country for more than 180 days need to apply for the temporary or permanent residence visa. However, some visitors settle in the country without applying for temporary or permanent residence by taking advantage of the tourist visa. They simply enter and settle in the country using the tourist visa. Once the 180-day period allowed by the tourist visa is nearing its expiry, they leave the country for a few days and come back, at which point they are issued with another tourist visa allowing them to stay for another six months. Foreigners who opt to follow this route instead of applying for residency must keep making these border runs every 180 days.

While you have the option of living in the country with a tourist visa and making border runs every 180 days, it is far better to apply for a residency visa if you are planning to settle in the country for an extended period of time. Having a residency visa makes your stay legal and grants you some additional rights that do not come with a tourist visa. There are two types of Mexican residency visas.

Temporary Residence Visa

If you want to live in Mexico for a period of more than 180 days but less than 4 years, you should apply for the temporary residency visa. While this visa allows you to live in the country for up to 4 years, it is good to note that you cannot get a 4-year temporary residency visa. Instead, it is issued for one year at a time. As the one-year period approaches its expiry, you can renew the temporary residency for an extra year and so on, up to the fourth year. Once your renewal for the fourth year expires, you will either need to leave the country or apply for a permanent residency visa. Fortunately, converting the temporary residency visa into a permanent residency visa is usually an easy process. Actually, it is much easier to apply for a temporary residency visa and convert it to permanent residency than directly applying for a permanent residency visa.

The temporary residency visa allows you to do some things that you might not be able to do with a tourist visa, such as opening a bank account, buying and registering a car with Mexican plates, importing household goods duty-free, bringing a vehicle with foreign plates into Mexico temporarily, coming and leaving Mexico as you please, and the possibility of upgrading to permanent residency after four years.

It is also good to note that there are a number of things that foreigners with a temporary residency visa cannot do, such as voting or owning land near the beach or the border. If a person with a temporary residency visa wants to work in Mexico, they have to apply for a "permission to work" visa. To be granted permission to work, you need to prove that you have actually received a job offer and pay the "permission to work" visa fee.

To apply for a temporary residency visa, you start by visiting the website of the closest Mexican Consulate in your home country. Note that, except under very special circumstances, you cannot apply for the temporary residency visa in Mexico. You have to do it at a Mexican consulate outside Mexico. Once you visit the website of the closest Mexican Consulate in your home country, find the immigration section and fill the online application form. The form is in Spanish, therefore you might need the services of an interpreter if you don't understand Spanish. After the form is processed, the consulate will email you to schedule an appointment for your in-person interview. Information regarding the documents you need to carry with you to the interview will be available on the website.

During the interview, an officer of the consulate will go through your documents and ask you a couple of questions regarding your current status, and why you want to move to Mexico. Before being approved for the temporary visa, you have to prove your economic insolvency. In other words, you must prove that you have a steady income or sufficient savings to sustain yourself for the duration you will be living in Mexico. For the temporary residency visa, you must prove that you have savings of over $27,000 or a monthly income of $1620 per month, plus an extra $540 per month for every person who depends on you, such as a spouse, kids, or elderly parents. Financial requirements for the permanent residency visa are a bit higher. If everything checks out, the decision to grant you the temporary residency visa can be made on the spot, in which case you might need to wait for just a day or two to receive your visa.

After you receive the visa, the first step of getting temporary residency is complete. This visa expires in 180 days, which means you have to arrive in Mexico before the 180 days are over, else you will have to start the whole process again. Once you arrive in Mexico, you will have 30 days to visit a local immigration office and complete the process by applying for an official residency card. If the 30 days pass before going through the process, your visa will become invalid, and you will be forced to leave the country and start the whole process again. Note that you become a legal resident of Mexico after receiving the official residency card.

Permanent Residency Visa

If you want to become a permanent resident or a Mexican citizen, or if you have stayed in the country as a temporary resident for four years and need to extend your stay, you need to apply for the permanent residency visa. It is not compulsory to have been a temporary resident before applying for a permanent residency. It is possible to directly apply for the permanent residency, provided you meet the stipulated requirements.

In order to be eligible for permanent residency, you need to meet one of the following conditions:

- You must have close family ties to someone who is already a citizen or permanent resident of Mexico.
- You must be a retiree applying for retirement status, in which case you must provide proof that you have sufficient savings, assets, or monthly income to support yourself.
- You must have lived in the country as a temporary resident for 4 consecutive years.
- You must have lived in the country as a temporary resident for 2 consecutive years, provided the temporary residency was granted on the basis of marriage to a Mexican citizen or a foreigner with permanent residency in Mexico.
- You must be applying for permanent residency through political asylum or through humanitarian grounds.

In order to be granted permanent residency, you also have to prove economic insolvency. In this case, you need to have savings of at least $108,000 or a monthly income of $2,700, plus an extra $540 for each person that will depend on you, such as a spouse, kids, or elderly parents. Once you receive the permanent residency card, you will be able to enter and leave the country just like any other Mexican citizen.

With a permanent residency visa, you get to enjoy all the rights that are extended to Mexican citizens, except the right to vote. The permanent residency visa has no expiry date, which means that you don't have to worry about renewing the visa now and then. The permanent residency visa also allows you to work in Mexico without having to apply for the "permission to work" visa. However, as a permanent resident, you are still not allowed to own land near the beach or a border or to import vehicles with foreign plates.

Citizenship

It is also possible for a foreigner to apply for and be granted Mexican citizenship, through the process of naturalization. Typically, anyone applying for a Mexican citizenship should already have acquired permanent residence in the country. However, there are some special conditions when a foreigner can be granted citizenship without first acquiring permanent residency, such as when one is married to a Mexican citizen, when one is the biological parent of someone who is a Mexican citizen by birth, or is a direct descendant of someone who is a Mexican citizen by birth.

In order to be granted Mexican citizenship, applicants must undertake a test which they have to pass before being granted citizenship. The test evaluates your knowledge of Mexican history, culture, politics, geography, and gastronomy. If you fail the test, you can attempt it 2 more times within the same 1 year period. If you still fail after three attempts, you will have to wait for 12 months before attempting the test again. The whole process of applying for and being granted Mexican citizenship takes about 6 to 8 months.

The CURP Card

If you intend to live in Mexico for an extended period and have already received your temporary or permanent residency visa, you also need to apply for a CURP card. CURP stands for *"Clave Única de Registro de Población,"* or the Unique Population Registry Code in English. This is a card with a unique number that is issued to everyone living in Mexico, both citizens and foreigners, and acts as a proof of identity. It is similar to the United States' Social Security Number.

You will need the CURP card in order to do various things within the country, such as applying for a Mexican driver's license, applying for a tax identification number and filing your taxes, applying for employment, opening a bank account, starting a business, registering a vehicle in the country, or accessing any other government services. For retirees living in Mexico, you will also need the CURP card in order to get enrolled on the INAPAM program, a special program that provides people above the age of 60 with discounts for several services across the country, such as plane and bus tickets, medical services, restaurants, and so on.

Fortunately, obtaining the CURP card is pretty straightforward. You only need to walk to the nearest immigration office with the original and a copy of your passport, the original and a copy of your residency visa (temporary or permanent), and your CURP request letter. You will not be required to pay any fees to receive the CURP card.

Chapter Three: The Cost Of Living In Mexico

If you are planning to move and settle in Mexico, it is important to understand how much it will cost you to live in the country. This is a crucial part of planning your move and determining whether making the move is a good thing to do. After all, what is the point of moving to a new country if you are going to be struggling to survive over there?

Fortunately, as we saw in chapter one, one of the main benefits of moving to Mexico is that you will get to enjoy a significantly lower cost of living. The US Dollar is fairly strong against the Mexican Peso, which means that foreigners coming to Mexico from most developed countries will be able to enjoy a fairly high living standard at a fraction of the cost they would have spent in their home countries. With the median household income in Mexico being slightly above a tenth of the median household income in the US, you can expect that the majority of your living needs will also be relatively cheap, even without considering the difference between the two countries' currencies. For instance, you might find that you are able to buy a pound of fruits such as avocados for just one dollar when one dollar back at home would have only gotten you just one avocado.

Of course, the benefits to be gained from Mexico's lower cost of living will depend on your lifestyle, your needs, your tastes, where in Mexico you choose to live, whether you rent or buy your home, and so on. For instance, someone who chooses to live in one of the rural towns will enjoy a lower cost of living compared to someone who opts for the big cities or the popular beach resort cities. Similarly, if you move to Mexico but insist on buying luxury items and imported goods, you will probably pay the same price you would have paid for them back home or even more.

Therefore, while life is definitely cheaper in Mexico, the extent to which you get to enjoy this reduced cost of living will ultimately depend on your decisions. Below, we'll take a look at the cost of some of the most basic things in Mexico.

Groceries And Food

Most of the grocery items you will buy in Mexican markets and grocery stores are grown locally rather than imported, which means that the prices are way lower than you would get in the United States. You can expect to pay less than half of what you would pay for the same groceries back at home. In addition, depending on where in Mexico you choose to live, you might have access to vendors and smaller markets, where the products are even cheaper than you would get at the grocery store at the mall. Most expats in the country will easily survive on a grocery budget of less than $200 per person per month. If you are not particularly extravagant, you can even survive on a monthly grocery budget of $100.

If you prefer eating out instead of cooking at home, you don't have to worry either, since most places are fairly cheap. For instance, in Mexico City, you can get very tasty and hearty meals for about $5 in neighborhood food courts and restaurants. If you decide to eat at the street-side stalls and food carts where a majority of locals prefer, you will pay way less. A three-course dinner at a mid-range restaurant in the heart of Mexico City will cost you about $15 on average. Note that these are price averages for Mexico City, the Mexican capital city. In smaller cities and towns, you can eat out for way less than that.

Entertainment And Social Life

Most Mexican cities and towns have a very vibrant culture and an exciting nightlife, and if you are anything like most expats, I'm sure you will want to go out and experience what the entertainment and social life feels like in Mexico. Fortunately, whether you want to enjoy a movie or a couple of drinks with friends, you can do this in Mexico without any serious damage to your wallet. For instance, you can grab two movie tickets for just $8. A cup of coffee in a nice restaurant will set you back about $2. For a beer, you can expect to pay just $1, while a cocktail at a nice bar will just cost you about $5 or less.

Transportation

Mexico has quite an extensive public transport network that is quite affordable and provides users with multiple options for moving around. In cities like Mexico City, Monterrey, and Guadalajara, you can get around on the metro system. In other cities, you can get around using mini buses known as peseros, or taxis, which are very easy to find. Most local fares will cost you around 50 cents per mile. In Mexico, you can even negotiate the price of your taxi before you commute to get a more favorable price. You can also move around your city or town in a three-wheeled taxis referred to as moto taxi (these are known as tuk-tuks in other countries), which are quite cheap. To travel across the country, you can use buses or travel by air. Air tickets for local travel are relatively cheap. For instance, if you book your flight early enough, you can travel from Mexico City to Cancun for as low as $60.

Housing

Like most other things, housing is pretty affordable in Mexico compared to countries like the United States. Of course, the prices will vary depending on where you choose to stay. For instance, if you live in Mexico City, right in the city center, you can expect to pay around $500 per month for a one-bedroom apartment, and about $1,100 for a three bedroom condo. If you opt for some smaller cities, you can get a two-bedroom apartment for around $350 or less. For instance, I have a gringo friend who pays $200 per month for a large, 2 bedroom apartment, inclusive of internet and all utilities, just 10 minutes away from central Oaxaca. The best part is that some of many of these apartments will be fully furnished. If you opt to buy instead of renting, you can easily purchase a fairly sized house for about $200,000–or less.

Utilities are equally cheap in Mexico. If you are using electricity moderately, you can expect to pay a monthly power bill of less than $50. However, if you live in areas that require frequent use of air conditioning, the costs can quickly skyrocket. Connection to high-speed internet and cable TV (which are usually bundled together) will cost you about $40 every month. Sometimes, however, the cost of internet and cable TV might be included in your monthly rent. Calling on a prepaid cell phone will set you back about 6 cents per minute. Cell phone companies also have some great affordable packages where you get a phone and unlimited talk time for a fixed price, just like back in the US. House services are also fairly cheap, owing to the low labor costs. For instance, you can hire a gardener or a maid for about $5 per hour. If you own a modest home, your annual property taxes will probably not exceed $200. Yes, that's per year.

Other Expenses

You will find that the cost of most of the other things you might need, such as clothing, household cleaning products, personal grooming products, and so on will also be quite affordable. However, this is only applicable if you opt for local products. If you insist on buying the same brands you are used to back at home, or if you decide to do your shopping at places like Walmart and Costco, where items are priced based on the dollar, your expenses will be similar to what you spend back at home, if not more. You will also find that healthcare is also fairly affordable in Mexico. In Mexico, you can expect to spend less than half of what you would ordinarily spend on healthcare back in the United States.

Overall Cost Of Living

Overall, living in Mexico is so much cheaper than living in the United States, Canada, or other developed countries. Of course, once in Mexico, your cost of living will depend on where you decide to settle down. If you go for areas like Puerto Vallarta, Riviera Maya, San, Miguel de Allende, Los Cabos, and other areas that are popular with tourists and expats, you can expect your cost of living to be a bit higher, even if it might still seem low compared to US or Canadian cities. On the other hand, if you opt for places such as Oaxaca, Monterrey, or Colima, you will really feel the benefits of a lower cost of living. Before settling, you can connect with other gringos living in the areas you are considering getting a better idea of the cost of living within the area, as well as to learn some tips that will help you save your money.

Chapter Four: Making Sense Of Money In Mexico

If you are only used to dealing with on currency, dealing with a new currency can a bit daunting at first, especially when it comes to converting between your home currency and the new currency. Unless you are used to dealing with Mexican currency before, it is inevitable that you will go through similar challenges when you first move to Mexico. Sometimes, I have even seen gringos who are so confused by Mexican currency that they end up placing a large wad of money on the counter and asking the shop attendant to take whatever amount is appropriate. To avoid such confusion when it comes to paying for goods and services, it is important to be a little familiar with Mexican currency before you make the move. In this chapter, I will teach you everything you need to know about *dinero* while in Mexico. Don't look so flustered, *dinero* is Spanish for money.

The Mexican Peso

The official currency in Mexico is known as the Mexican Peso, which is officially abbreviated as MXN. Just like the dollar is made up of 100 cents, the peso is made up of 100 Mexican centavos. The bills of Mexican currency come in various colors, based on the denomination of the bill. Different denomination bills also have different pictures of some of the most important people in Mexican history.

There are six denominations of peso bills: 20, 50, 100, 200, 500 and 1000 peso bills. The 20 and 50 peso notes are made of polymer plastic and are therefore unlikely to get spoilt or tear even if they get wet. The higher denominations, on the other hand, are printed on some special textured paper. You can tell apart a genuine peso bill from a counterfeit one by checking whether it has a watermark showing the denomination and the face of the person on the bill. Aside from the peso bills, Mexican currency also uses coins, which come in the following denominations: 10 centavos, 20 centavos, 50 centavos, and 1, 5, 10, and 20 pesos. In most of Mexico, pesos are represented by the symbol "$" while centavos are represented by the symbol "¢".

How Much Are Your Dollars Worth In Mexico?

One of the advantages of spending dollars in Mexico is that the dollar gives you so much spending power against the Mexican peso. At the time of writing this book (June 2019), 1 US dollar is equivalent to 19 Mexican pesos. One Canadian dollar, on the other hand, is equivalent to 14 Mexican pesos. Since the Mexican peso is the currency on forex markets, its value against the dollar keeps changing on a daily basis, so you need to keep yourself up to date with the daily exchange rates. You can easily do this by downloading a currency conversion app on your smartphone.

While most of the areas that are popular with tourists and expats will accept US dollars, it is more preferable to carry pesos. This is because when paying using dollars at establishments such as shops, hotels, and restaurants, you might be charged a higher exchange rate than you would be charged when exchanging your dollars for pesos at a bank or exchange bureau, or when withdrawing pesos from the ATM. For instance, if the exchange rate is 19.07 pesos to 1 dollar, some establishments might bring this down to about 17 or 16 pesos to 1 dollar.

Considering that dollars and pesos are both represented by the "$" symbol, sometimes gringos might be left confused whether the prices are in dollars or pesos. To avoid such confusion, businesses will sometimes write dollars as DLLs and Mexican pesos as either MXP or MN, which stands for *"Moneda Nacional,"* or national currency. In these cases, a price of 100 dollars will be written as $100 DLLS, while the price of 100 pesos will be written as $100 MN or $100 MXP. However, in case the price does not distinguish between dollars and pesos, and it seems too high, it is probably meant to be in pesos, though it is best to confirm with the attendant or waiter before ordering. When going into the more rural areas, you should carry pesos with you, because people and businesses in these places might not accept dollars.

Getting Change

One peculiar thing you might notice about Mexico is that getting change can be quite a problem. If you buy something worth just a few pesos from a small shop or street-side vendor with a 500 or 1000 peso note, it might take them a while to get the change. Sometimes, they might even be forced to walk to the next shop or stall to request for change. Some won't even sell to you or offer you their services once they realize that you have a 500 or 1000 peso note. To avoid having to wait several minutes as a shop attendant or vendor looks for change, get in the habit of carrying smaller denomination bills and coins with you. You can then use these when paying shopkeepers, taxi drivers, convenience stores, small restaurants, roadside vendors, buses, public toilets, and so on. Having the small denomination notes and coins also comes in handy when you need to tip waiters, and those who bag your groceries at the supermarket. Only use notes above 200 pesos at bigger establishments where getting change won't be a problem.

Where To Exchange Your Money

You have several options when it comes to exchanging your dollars for Mexican pesos. Your first option is to exchange your money at the bank. There are several large Mexican banks as well as international banks that will be willing to convert your dollars into pesos at a fair rate. However, most banks will add a 4-5% spread to the market rates, so the exchange rate will be a little inflated compared to the market rate.

Another great option is to exchange your money at the exchange bureau, which is locally referred to as *Casa de Cambio*. You will find many of them along the streets, near hotels, and in shopping malls. Exchanging your money at exchange bureaus is somewhat more convenient than banks, since they operate for more hours than banks (some will even be open at night), and you won't experience the long queues you might have to deal with at the bank. The exchange rates offered by exchange bureaus are also quite fair, though you will get a slightly better rate at the bank. You can easily find an exchange bureau by searching for the terms *"exchange"* or *"Cambio"* on Google Maps.

You also have the option of exchanging your dollars for Mexican pesos at the airport or at a hotel, though I do not recommend this option, because you will generally get a very low rate for your dollars. It is also important to note that there is a cap to the number of dollars you can exchange for Mexican pesos per day or per month. These regulations were put in place from 2010 with the aim of reducing organized crime and money laundering. Because of these laws, you will also be required to provide some of your passport or some other form of identification (such as your CURP card) while converting your dollars to pesos. This makes it possible for the government to monitor the amount of money you are exchanging.

ATMs in Mexico

You can also withdraw Mexican pesos directly from your foreign bank account through most of the several ATMs that are scattered all over most Mexican cities and towns. The exchange rates offered when withdrawing pesos from ATMs are quite favorable, though the bank will charge you a transaction fee for using the ATM. I'd recommend using ATMs operated by large banks such as Banco Santander, Banamex, HSBC, and Banorte. This is because smaller banks might charge you significantly high fees for directly withdrawing pesos from your foreign bank account.

While finding ATMs is easy in most of Mexico, I would also advise you to carry enough cash with you whenever you travel to the rural areas of the country, since finding ATMs in the rural areas might be a bit difficult. You should also avoid withdrawing money from ATMs around payday (the 15th and 30th) since you will most likely encounter very long queues at the ATMs. In addition, thieves are more alert at these times of the month because they expect many people to be carrying huge amounts of cash. It is also advisable to be very vigilant when using ATMs at all times. Avoid street-side ATMs and opt for those in a well-lit and highly populated or safe places, such as banks or malls.

Are Debit And Credit Cards Accepted In Mexico?

In the large cities and in areas that are popular with tourists and expats, credit and debit cards are widely accepted. You can use credit and debit cards to pay for airline tickets, store purchases, big hotels and restaurants, and so on. Some gas stations also accept credit card payments, though it is best to confirm before pumping. The most commonly accepted cards in Mexico are American Express, MasterCard and Visa. While the rates are fairly favorable when paying through a credit card, it is important to note that some establishments will add a 5-7% surcharge for payments made via card.

It is also good to keep in mind that most street-side food stalls, neighborhood restaurants, small shops and vendors, taxis and buses, and other small businesses will not accept credit card payments, so it is always advisable to have some cash with you.

Tipping In Mexico

Like most other places, wait staff in most Mexican restaurants will be expecting you to leave a tip. A typical tip is about 10–20% of what you are paying, depending on how good the service was. Most wait staff in Mexican restaurants receive very low wages, and a small tip will make a huge difference to whoever is serving you. Aside from wait staff at restaurants, other people who might be expecting a tip include tour guides (about $50 - $100 MXN), people who assist you with your luggage (a few pesos are enough), staff who clean your hotel room (about $50 - $100 MXN per day), and people who help you pack what you have bought at the grocery store ($5 - $10 MXN). Unlike in places like Canada, Mexican taxi and shuttle drivers won't be expecting any tip, unless they help with your luggage, in which case you can tip them anywhere between $20 and $50 pesos.

With the above tips, I believe you are not going to have much trouble dealing with dinero during your stay in Mexico. Of course, the longer you stay in the country, the more conversant you will become with the local currency and money matters in general.

Chapter Five: Living In Mexico: To Rent Or To Buy?

One of the most common questions I get from foreigners looking to move and settle in Mexico is whether to rent or buy your own property in the country. While this is definitely a very important thing, it is not as straightforward as you might be tempted to think. The decision between renting and buying will depend on several factors, such as your financial capabilities, your long-term goals, your experiences within the country, and so on. However, each of the two options has its benefits. Let's take a closer look at the two options.

Renting A Property In Mexico

If you don't have the financial muscle to purchase a home, or if you have not made a final decision as to where you want to settle permanently, renting is your best option. Renting is also a good option if you want to get a feel of the real estate and the local community before you buy. Fortunately, finding a rental property in Mexico is quite easy. A high number of Mexican families living in the cities live in rental properties, therefore there is no shortage of houses to rent, from small, bare-bones apartments to huge, fully furnished homes. In addition, the rents in Mexico are fairly affordable.

Below are a few listed advantages of renting a property in Mexico.

1. Fewer Responsibilities

When you choose to live in a rented property, you won't have to handle most of the responsibilities that come with the property. I'm talking about things such as maintaining the property and fixing anything that might need to be repaired, such as plumbing and wiring problems, leaky roofs, faulty water heaters, and so on. All these are the responsibility of the landlord. In addition, you won't have to worry about paying taxes for the property.

2. Friendly On Your Pocket

Buying a property is a sizeable investment. Even though buying a house is a lot cheaper in Mexico compared to the United States or Canada, not everyone will have this much money to spend at a go. Renting, on the other hand, requires that you only pay the rental fee and an advance deposit for the first one or two months. Therefore, if you find an apartment whose rent is $350 per month, you will only need $700 to start living in the house (one month deposit plus that month's rent). In addition, rental prices are much lower compared to mortgage repayments.

3. Short Term Commitment

Most rental contracts in Mexico are short-term oriented. Most are renewed on a monthly basis (by paying the rent), while a few landlords offer one or two-year contracts. Having such a short-term contract gives you freedom and mobility. If you don't like something about the apartment/house, you can easily move to another one the next month, instead of remaining there for a longer period while waiting for your contract to expire. This is important because, in some cases, there might be some defects in the building or something you don't like about the neighborhood that you only discover after moving in.

Finding The Right Place To Rent

Finding a rental property in Mexico is pretty easy. Most agents list their vacant units in newspapers or online forums, so all you need to do is simply browse the paper or property forums. If you find something that sounds like what you are looking for, get in touch with the owner or agent and make an appointment to go and view the property. If it is to your liking, you can go ahead and sign the contract, pay a month's rent and one month's advance deposit and move into the unit.

Aside from listings in newspapers and online forums, many landlords will also put up "For Rent" signs on the windows of buildings or outside their gates in case they have vacant units. Therefore, if you find a neighborhood that appeals to you, walk around the neighborhood for a few days to see if you will find any vacant units. If you find a "For Rent" sign in a place you like, call the number posted on the sign, and someone will be available to show you the vacant unit.

Word of mouth is another great tool when it comes to finding rental properties in Mexico. If you find an area or neighborhood that looks appealing to you, walk into neighborhood stores near and ask the owners if they are aware of any vacant rental properties. Similarly, if you have friends living within the area, you can ask them to let you know in case they come across a vacant unit.

The Rental Market In Mexico

It is good to note that there are two major categories of rental markets in Mexico. The first one is focused on tourists who prefer staying in a rental property instead of a hotel. Such rental properties usually accommodate visitors looking for short-term stays, typically a few days to a couple of weeks, and are therefore more expensive than long-term rentals. Most properties within this category are fully furnished and come complete with services such as telephone, internet, and cable TV, as well as kitchen supplies. Most will also provide cleaning or maintenance cost. All this is covered in the cost of renting the property. While these are more expensive, it is still possible to negotiate for a slightly better deal if you intend to stay in the apartment for an extended period.

The second and larger category of the rental market comprises properties that are focused on locals and residents and are meant for long term stays. These may either come as furnished or unfurnished, though most are usually unfurnished. This means that you will have to factor the cost of purchasing furniture, appliances and other furnishings before moving into the house or apartment.

Alternatively, if you just moved to Mexico and have not found a nice place to rent or buy, but don't want to stay in a hotel, you also have the option of staying in an Airbnb. If you are not conversant with Airbnb, it is an app that allows people looking for accommodation with people with unoccupied houses or rooms looking to host guests. Most Airbnb is fully furnished. You simply arrive with your bags and settle in. In most cases, staying in an Airbnb is much cheaper than staying in a fully furnished rental apartment that is targeted at tourists. Still, Airbnbs are meant for short-term stays and will, therefore, be more expensive than renting an apartment.

Renting a property by foreigners in Mexico is hassle-free since there are no government restrictions regarding the same. Unlike many other countries, rental prices in Mexico can sometimes be negotiated. If you like a unit but feel that it is a bit more expensive than you were looking for, you can ask the landlord or agent if the price is flexible. When negotiating, you will have an added advantage if you know Spanish. If your Spanish is not fluent, bring a friend over with you to help you negotiate.

Buying A Property In Mexico

A lot of expats like the idea of owning property in Mexico, and if you have no financial limitations, buying has better benefits in the long term compared to renting. Unlike the past where most foreigners had to buy property in Mexico with cash, today the interest rates on property financing have come down significantly, making it even easier for foreigners to buy property in Mexico. Some advantages of buying instead of renting include:

Peace Of Mind

Owning your own place gives you peace of mind because you don't have to deal with other people, such as landlords or agents. This is especially important in Mexico, where a landlord has the liberty to raise the monthly rent for their rental property if they so wish. When you own your own place, you are confident that you will never have to deal with such issues.

It Is An Investment

Buying your own property is also a great investment, especially in a country like Mexico, which is rapidly growing a top tourist and retirement destination for expats. Property has the potential for financial appreciation and considering Mexico's fast-growing economy, a house you bought today could be worth a lot more in a few years' time.

In addition, buying a home, especially through bank financing, allows you to build your credit history in your new country. This will come in handy when you need banks to finance more of your projects. Even if you buy a house in Mexico with cash, the fact that you own property in the country is enough to give banks and financial institutions a feeling of confidence in case you need to access credit. Being a property owner in Mexico also significantly reduces the monthly income you need in order to be eligible for a permanent residency visa.

Greater Freedom

Having your own home also gives you the freedom to do as you please with the property. Unlike a rental property where you are not allowed to make any significant changes to the property, with your own home, you can do renovations, add improvements, and personalize it to suit your needs and tastes. Some renovations and improvements will even increase the value of the property. In addition, you have the option of letting out the property out in case you decide to go back to your home country, or in case you buy another property.

Restrictions For Foreigners Seeking To Buy Property

While foreigners with temporary or permanent residency visas are allowed to own property in Mexico, there are some restrictions. Specifically, foreigners are not allowed to directly own a residential property that is within 31 miles of the coastline or less than 62 miles from Mexico's border with another country. However, they can purchase such properties through a trust, where the bank acts as the trustee. In this case, the property will be legally owned by the bank, while the foreigner will be treated as the trust's beneficiary. As the beneficiary, the foreigner has the right to sell, mortgage, and lease the property, or pass the trust to an heir. Once created, a trust will remain good for 50 years, after which it has to be renewed.

Now that you have seen the advantages of renting vis-à-vis the advantages of buying your own property, the question still lingers, to buy or to rent? If you have the financial capability, buying is ultimately better. However, don't buy right away. Instead, I would advise you to rent for some time to get a feel of the neighborhood or city before you commit to buying.

Chapter Six: Where To Live In Mexico

Mexico is a vast country, and there is no shortage of great places to settle. Whether you prefer the beaches or the mountains, big cities or small towns, historical towns or modern resort towns, there is something for you. If you are planning to move and settle in Mexico, it is also important to get acquainted with the climate of the country, since this will probably influence where you end up settling. Therefore, before we get to some great places, you might want to settle in Mexico, let us first take a look at the different climatic regions in Mexico.

The Three Main Climate Zones In Mexico

In addition to its vast territory, Mexico also contains a very diverse geographical structure, from mountain ranges exceeding 10,000 feet above sea level to temperate highlands and coastal plains. The result of such a diverse topography is that the country has varied climate zones. Being aware of these climate zones before you settle is important since a place's climate will influence its characteristics, and ultimately, how well you end up liking the place.

Mexico's climate can be classified into three major zones, named in accordance with the geographical regions where the climate is most likely to be experienced. These are:

The Hot Lands

This climate zone consists of areas along Mexico's vast coastline, which range in altitude from sea level to about 2460 feet above sea level. Considering that the country has over 6000 miles of coastline, you can bet that the hot lands make up a sizeable portion of the country. The hot lands comprise both the areas along the Gulf of Mexico and the Pacific Coast, such as the coastal plains on the Baja California and the Baja California Sur, the Yucatan Peninsula, The Riviera Maya, and the area around the Isthmus of Tehuantepec, which lies between the States of Oaxaca and Veracruz to the west and Chiapas and Tabasco to the east. Some cities and towns that experience this climate include Cancun, Merida, Cabo San Lucas, Mazatlan, Playa Del Carmen, Puerto Vallarta, and so on.

Areas within the hot lands are warm throughout the year, though it can get very hot and humid at certain times of the year. If you are comfortable with the warm weather, these are the places for you.

The Temperate Lands

This climate zone consists of areas that lie between 2460 and 7550 feet above sea level. The areas that experience this type of climate are found inland, away from the beaches and flanking the mountain ranges. As you might have inferred from the name, the climate in these regions is mild and moderate climate all around the year. Sometimes, however, the temperate lands may get very cold, though it is nothing to compare with winters up north in the United States or Canada. Mexico's three big cities–Guadalajara, Mexico City, and Monterrey–lie within the temperate lands, as well as a majority of Mexico's attractive colonial cities, such as Campeche, Chihuahua, Guanajuato, Oaxaca, Puebla, and so on.

The Cold Lands

This climate zone consists of areas that exceed 7550 feet above sea level. These are the areas that are found within Mexico's mountain ranges, including the Sierra Madre Oriental, Sierra Madre

Occidental, and Sierra Madre del Sur. As the name suggests, these zones are very cold, and there are very few settled villages and towns at these very high altitudes. Most of the settlements in the high-altitude cold lands are inhabited by indigenous residents. Most foreigners only visit these settlements on tourist expeditions, rather than settling there.

Where To Settle In Mexico

Now that you are aware of the main climate zones in Mexico, let us take a look at some of the best cities and towns for foreigners wishing to settle in Mexico.

Cancun

Located at the most eastern tip of the Yucatan Peninsula, Cancun is a beach town along Mexico's coast on the Gulf of Mexico. Cancun is one of Mexico's top resort towns, despite the fact that half a century ago, it was a tiny fishing village with nothing to write home about. In 1974, it was targeted for development that turned the sleepy fishing village into a vibrant resort town with about 700,000 people. What attracts people to the town is it's amazing weather, amazing beaches, and beautiful vacation resorts. For expats looking to settle within Cancun, you get to enjoy the small-town feel while you can still access the high-end shopping and excellent restaurants that are usually associated with the bigger cities. The town is also very popular among tourists.

Playa Del Carmen

Located just an hour south of Cancun on the Riviera Maya, Playa del Carmen (simply known to locals as Playa) is another once a sleepy fishing village that has been transformed into a vibrant resort town. The Riviera Maya is the 125-mile long section of coast on the Yucatan Peninsula, between the towns of Tulum and Playa del Carmen. Playa del Carmen's claim to fame is a 1954 underwater documentary by Jacques Cousteau, which featured the Great Maya Reef just offshore the small village. Today, it is the place to be, attracting multitudes of tourists and foreign residents. At the moment, there are more than 10,000 foreigners residing within Playa del Carmen, including young couples and families, as well as retired people from the United States, Canada, and Europe.

One of the main attractions to the small town is the renowned La Quinta Avenida, a pedestrian street that runs alongside the beach and offers over 20 blocks of shops and fine restaurants. In addition, everyone will love the beautiful beaches that run alongside the breathtaking small town.

Tulum

Tulum lies a couple of miles south of Playa del Carmen. About a decade ago, there was nothing notable about Tulum. It can't be qualified to be called a town. It was just a handful of fishing shacks and a couple of cabins. Today, however, the small tranquil town has a population of about 18,000 people. The growth of Tulum can be attributed to tourism since there are a couple of natural attractions and ancient Mayan sites close to the town. Due to its tourism-oriented nature, most of the people in Tulum speak English, and it is quite easy to feel like you are in a first world country while in Tulum. It is the perfect place to settle in Mexico without losing touch with your home culture. However, owing to the high number of tourists who visit the town and its popularity with expats, Tulum is a bit expensive.

One of the things you will love most about Tulum is the weather. The place is warm throughout the year, and even in the coldest season, the temperatures will feel fairly warm compared to what you are used to at home. The beaches around Tulum are pristine, and the Caribbean waters are quite warm. The Great Mayan Reef, which is just offshore, makes Tulum a great place for snorkeling and diving. Oh, and if you are a golf player worried about abandoning your favorite game after settling in Tulum, you have nothing to worry about, because there are a couple of world-class courses within the vicinity. The town is also one of the safest places in Mexico.

Merida

This is another lovely city that lies on the northern part of the Yucatan peninsula. It is a vibrant city that is also the capital of the State of Yucatan and one of the most popular cities amongst expats from the United States, Canada, and Europe. One of the greatest things about Merida is that the city is a combination of hustle and bustle of city life and the laid back vibe of small beach towns. In the heart of the city, you will find fabulous restaurants, Mayan temples that were rebuilt into colonial-era churches and Cathedrals, a live theater, an English Language Library, parks, museums, and American stores like Costco and Walmart, while the warm, pristine beaches are just thirty minutes away from the heart of the city. If you want to travel, there is a major airport just outside the city.

Merida is very safe, and the cost of living there is much lower compared to towns like Tulum or Playa del Carmen. The city of Merida is an interesting cacophony of cultures, with influences from Mayan, Spanish, French, British, Dutch and Lebanese cultures. Merida (and the entire Yucatan peninsula) has some of the best food in Mexico, probably second after Oaxaca. The city also enjoys warm weather throughout the year. It is the perfect place if you want to live in a modern city but without the claustrophobia of big cities like Mexico City, and at the same time have beautiful beaches just a stone's throw away.

The cities and towns we discussed above are all located on the east coast. Let's now move on to the west coast where we have towns and cities like...

Puerto Peñasco

If you want to move to Mexico, but still remain within close proximity to the United States, Puerto Peñasco is the perfect place for you. Also referred to as Rocky Point, this seaside resort town, which lies near the topmost point of the Gulf of California, is just an hour away from the Mexican border with the state of Arizona in the United States. You can easily drive over from the United States to Puerto Peñasco, one of the reasons why the town has been a playground for Americans and Canadians for almost a century.

One of the greatest things you will love about Puerto Peñasco is its beautiful, broad and sandy beaches with very calm waters, as well as its all year round warm weather. Additionally, property prices are quite affordable in Puerto Peñasco, and there are lots of housing options. You can buy a two-bedroom condo near the beach for as low as $110,000.

Mazatlan

The resort city of Mazatlan lies on the beautiful Mexican Riviera, about midway along Mexico's Pacific coast. At some point, Mazatlan had fallen from its former graces, but within the last decade, it has undergone renovations and facelifts, making the beach resort city popular with tourists and expats once again. Today, the socially diverse city is home to modern sidewalk cafes, world-class restaurants and resorts, and a beautiful beachfront promenade. This, coupled with its historic sites, ancient cathedrals, miles of beautiful beaches and boardwalks, and its low cost of living compared to other cities in Mexico makes Mazatlan a gem for expats.

Puerto Vallarta

Before the 1950s, there was nothing spectacular about Puerto Vallarta. It was just one of the many small fishing villages along Mexico's Pacific coast. In the early 1960s, John Huston came to a seaside village just south of Puerto Vallarta to shoot the film "*The Night Of The Iguana.*" At the time, Richard Burton, who was the star in Huston's film, was in a romantic relationship with Elizabeth Taylor, another popular American actress. The paparazzi had followed the two down to Mexico, and in sharing their gossip, pictures of the couple in Puerto Vallarta started appearing in American newspapers, attracting American attention to the small village.

Seeing the increase of tourists to Puerto Vallarta, the Mexican government made heavy investments within the area, building roads, highways, and public utilities, with the aim of making Puerto Vallarta more attractive and accessible to tourists. Puerto Vallarta has remained a popular seaside resort ever since then, attracting both tourists and expats looking to settle in Mexico. Anyone moving to the city will enjoy its beautiful beaches, galleries, gourmet restaurants, and a wide range of cultural activities, including classical concerts, films, plays, and jazz. You will also find lots of amazing properties on the lush, green hills just outside the city, with some of the best ocean views.

Ixtapa

Ixtapa is another awesome beach town along Mexico's western coast, located a couple of minutes from the resort city of Zihuatanejo.

Ixtapa has the vibe of a small but modern resort town. Initially, Ixtapa was nothing more than a plantation of coconuts. In the 1970s, the Mexican Tourist Board was looking for a location on the west coast to build another resort town like Cancun on the east coast, and they settled on Ixtapa. The government invested in the town and turned it into a modern resort with world-class luxury hotels, good infrastructure and amenities, and awesome resort villages. With its stunning beaches and natural scenery, with the majestic Sierra Madre Occidental Mountains acting as a breathtaking backdrop, there is nothing not to love about Ixtapa.

Huatulco

This is another beach community that is located along the Pacific Coast, with the Sierra Madre Mountains providing an amazing backdrop to the town. Huatulco is a master-planned community that combines tourist and residential development with ecological conservation. One of the major advantages of Huatulco is that it has more of a small-town feel compared to other resort cities that are popular with expats, such as Cancun or Playa del Carmen. At the same time, you won't lack any of the modern amenities that you are used to. You can easily get to Huatulco by plane from Mexico City. It is just an hour's flight.

The cities and towns discussed above are all located along the beach. However, not everyone wants to settle near the beach. Some expats prefer settling in the temperate lands of Mexico's hinterland. If this sounds like you, don't feel left out. Some great places to settle in Mexico's hinterland include…

Guadalajara

Located about 350 miles west of Mexico City, Guadalajara is the second biggest city in Mexico and the capital of the state of Jalisco. It is the birthplace of tequila and the famous Mariachi music. If you want the excitement of living in a big city but don't want to deal with overcrowding, pollution, and traffic of Mexico City, Guadalajara is the place for you. Guadalajara is a modern, progressive city and a technological hub that has even been nicknamed the "Silicon Valley of Mexico." The city, which is home to four million people, has a vibrant culture with diverse cuisine and awesome restaurants and an interesting bar scene with a budding craft beer scene. Guadalajara enjoys a humid subtropical climate, with temperatures that remain mildly warm (not as warm as coastal towns) throughout the year.

San Miguel de Allende

This remarkably beautiful town lies at the heart of Mexico. Located in the state of Guanajuato, San Miguel de Allende lies almost an equal distance from Veracruz on the Gulf of Mexico and Puerto Vallarta on the Pacific Coast. The sociable colonial town, which is home to thousands of expats, lies at an altitude of 6,200 feet above sea level. The temperatures in San Miguel de Allende are awesome, with warm days and cool nights.

San Miguel de Allende was founded by the Spanish back in the 1500s as an important town in the Mexican Silver trade. This explains the Spanish architecture on its beautiful colonial homes and cobblestone streets. The town is fairly level, which makes it great for walking and cycling. There are numerous shopping venues and first-class restaurants in this beautiful city, and it has even been classified as one of Mexico's Pueblo Magicos (more on this later in this chapter). I can promise that you will never regret settling in San Miguel de Allende.

Guanajuato

The city of Guanajuato is another beautiful colonial city within the state of Guanajuato, though it feels more authentic than San Miguel de Allende. It is also the capital of the state of Guanajuato and is home to about 170,000 people. The city lies at an altitude of about 6,600 feet above sea level, cradled in the mountains of the Sierra de Guanajuato. Guanajuato City enjoys comfortable weather, but considering that it is located in the mountains, sometimes it does get a bit cool at night.

While there are not as many expats in Guanajuato City as compared to San Miguel de Allende, it is still a great city for expats with everything you might need. The fact that there are not as many expats also means that you get to enjoy the Spanish culture with less expat influence.

Most of the streets within Guanajuato city are narrow, winding and cobblestone-paved, while some even have stairs to get to the higher parts of the city which means a lot of the streets are not passable by car. Vehicle traffic mostly uses the city's underground thoroughfares. The narrow streets of Guanajuato are dotted with theaters, museums, historic monuments, as well as sidewalk cafes and markets, which will give you the feel of having traveled back in time. However, you won't miss any of the modern amenities you are used to. Many of the buildings–especially the colonial era churches and mansions–within the city are built using green and pink sandstone, giving the city a beautiful look that has earned the city the title of the most beautiful city in Mexico.

Alamos

Alamos is a small colonial town in the state of Sonora, with a population of about 25,000 people. The town is nestled in an inland valley, with mountains surrounding it on all sides. Alamos grew back in the 1600s following the discovery of silver in the area surrounding the town. Wealthy silver merchants built huge colonial homes and mansions throughout the town, which still define the town to date. One of the things you will love about Alamos is that it is a very safe and fairly walkable city. The town also has an active, welcoming and cohesive expat community, with many of the expats involved in artistic and creative endeavors–writers, artists, poets, musicians, and so on. If you want a small-town alternative to cities like Oaxaca, Guanajuato or San Miguel de Allende, Alamos might be a good option for you.

Ajijic, Lake Chapala

Ajijic is a scenic town that is located on the shores of Lake Chapala in the state of Jalisco, several miles south of Guadalajara, and about 30 minutes' drive from Guadalajara International airport. The small lakeside paradise is a hotspot for American and Canadian expats. During winter, expats make up almost 50% of the population in Ajijic. Owing to the high number of expats, there is a higher variety of restaurants and shops in Ajijic than you would find in similar small towns in Mexico. The fact that the town is also close to Guadalajara means that expats can be tucked in a unique natural setting, away from the urban sprawl, while at the same time being close enough to the big city.

Owing to the high number of expats, life is not very much different from back home. You can comfortably live in Ajijic without ever needing to speak Spanish. Still, the cost of living is a lot lower compared to the big Mexican cities or the resort towns along the coast, such as Cancun or Playa del Carmen. In addition, Ajijic is very safe. You are also going to love the weather. The fact that the town is lies at a high altitude means the temperatures are much lower than they would be at sea level, while Lake Chapala (the largest lake in Mexico) helps to regulate temperatures, making the area less hot in summer and less cold in winter.

Oaxaca

This list would not be complete without mentioning the city of Oaxaca, the capital of the state of Oaxaca. There are a lot of things to love about living in Oaxaca. The weather is warm throughout the year, the food is awesome (Oaxaca has the best food in the whole of Mexico), there are lots of fantastic restaurants, there are some very nice parks, there is tons of culture, the people are very friendly, there are several markets where you can buy groceries at very low prices, there are some very nice craft beer bars, and the city generally has a very nice vibe. Oaxaca is generally very safe, and there are numerous nice little neighborhoods that are great for expats. You will really love it in Oaxaca. Oh, and if you feel like heading to the beach, the beachside towns of Merida and Cancun are about one hour's flight away.

Pueblos Magicos

While the towns and cities I covered above are some of the most popular with tourists and expats in Mexico, that's not all there is to Mexico. A great deal of Mexico's charm lies in what is known as Pueblos Magicos (Spanish for magical towns). Pueblos Magicos are small towns and villages that are off the beaten path, hidden among the country's mountains, foothills, and coastal plains.

The Pueblos Magicos program was a government initiative by the Mexican Ministry of Tourism that was developed to promote Mexico's rich history and cultural heritage through small towns that were previously overlooked. The pueblos magicos are a selection of such small towns that are exceptionally special owing to their cultural richness, historical significance, natural treasures, and gastronomical richness. Each of these magical towns has a unique characteristic for which it is recognized.

Currently, there are 111 towns and villages covered under the pueblos magicos program. Examples of some of these magical towns include Mitla in Oaxaca, Bacalar in Quintana Roo, Patzcuaro in Michoacán, Tequila in Jalisco, Papantla in Veracruz, Dolores Hidalgo in Guanajuato, Tepoztlan in Morelos, Huasca de Ocampo in Hidalgo, Bernal in Queretaro, Comala in Colima, Todos Santos in Baja California Sur, Izamal in Yucatan, and so on. If you want to settle in simple, amazing towns, away from the hustle and bustle of the big cities and tourist towns, then the pueblos magicos are the place for you.

As you have seen from this chapter, there is no shortage of nice places to settle in Mexico. If anything, you might actually be left confused as to where you should settle, with all these amazing cities and towns to choose from. Ultimately, it all comes down to your priorities, preferences and personal taste. However, regardless of your preferences or budget, you will definitely find a suitable place for you in Mexico.

Chapter Seven: Crime, Drug Cartels And Safety In Mexico

I want us to do a little experiment right now. Grab the phone and tell someone close to you–a parent, a relative, or a close friend–that you want to move to Mexico, and listen to their greatest concern. Most times, people will respond to this information with questions like: Is it really safe in Mexico? Have you heard of the drug war in Mexico? Aren't you afraid of getting kidnapped or even killed? Why would you want to go to Mexico, that's the most dangerous country on the planet? Are you out of your mind? Do you care not about your safety?

Yes, that's right. When you tell people that you want to move to Mexico, one of their first questions will always have something to do safety. The concerns about safety in Mexico can be greatly attributed to the sensationalist reporting by the media about the drug war that has been going on in Mexico for more than a decade now. Aside from the drug war, the media also propagates any crime that is ever committed in Mexico as a reason to be afraid for your safety in Mexico, even if these crimes would not affect you in any way as a tourist or expat. Trust me, Mexico is a lot safer than the media makes it appear.

To show you how ridiculous it seems to write off the whole of Mexico as dangerous because of things like the drug war, lets for a minute consider the size of Mexico. Mexico is the 14th largest country in the world, with an area of 1.973 million kilometers squared. That is three times bigger than the whole of Texas, the second biggest state in the United States, and about 5 times bigger than California, the third biggest state in the United States. Now, if there was some violence in the small area near the western tip of Texas, would it really make sense saying that it is not safe to live in the rest of Texas? Not in the least bit. Therefore, you can imagine how ridiculous it is to claim that the whole of Mexico, which is three times bigger than Texas, is dangerous just because there are a few pockets of violence within the country. Actually, some areas that are popular with expats are more than 1000 miles from the areas that experience drug-related violence. You really wouldn't expect drug cartels to travel 1000 miles just to kidnap an expat.

What makes the claims about Mexico being dangerous even more preposterous is the fact that a majority of those who tell you that Mexico is not safe has never been to the country! If you ask them to give you specifics of the violence or what areas you need to avoid, they will stare at you blankly. This is because their fears are just driven by what they see in movies combined with the sensationalist reporting in the media and blogosphere. In truth, however, the majority of Mexico is relatively safe. Of the more than 130 million people who live in Mexico, the majority live regular lives, without being affected by the drug-related violence in any way.

Of course, this is not to say that Mexico is the safest country in the world. As an expat, if you want to remain safe, you will need to avoid certain areas and keep your wits around you. Below, let's take a look at what you need to know about drug-related violence and overall crime while in Mexico and how to keep yourself safe.

Drug-Related Violence In Mexico

Crime and violence related to the drug trade is the biggest concern for foreigners worried about their safety while in Mexico, so this is what I'll start by addressing.

Mexico finds itself in a somewhat tricky situation. Owing to the fact that it shares a large border with the United States, and the fact that it is still a developing country where corruption is rife, it is the perfect place to act as the last handover point for drugs from Latin America into the United States. Actually, according to a report by CNN, almost 90% of the cocaine sold in the United States gets into the country through Mexico. According to the same CNN report, Mexican drug cartels make between $20 and $30 billion per year from selling drugs in the United States.

From 2006, following the election of Felipe Calderon as president, the Mexican government started battling the drug cartels in an attempt to rid the country of the menace of drug trafficking. As the government cracks down on the cartels, the killing or arrest of cartel leaders creates voids in the control of cartel turfs, leading to battles between various cartels seeking to fill the void and take control of the billion dollar illegal drug trade. Therefore, the violence usually occurs among people involved with the drug trade, and rarely do innocent people get involved. According to CS Monitor, more than 90% of the people killed as a result of drug-related violence are people who were directly involved in the drug trade, while 7% of the deaths were officials of the Mexican government.

While the murders and gunfights resulting from the control for drug trafficking turfs make for sensationalist reporting by international media outlets and contribute to the fear that most foreigners have about moving to Mexico, they do not typically affect people who are not involved in the drug industry. Therefore, if you are thinking of moving to Mexico, drug-related crime and violence should not really be a concern for you, provided you avoid the areas where the cartels operate.

So, what areas should you avoid? Drug-related violence is most widespread in the northern parts of the country, near the border with the United States, and particularly within the states of Tamaulipas, Nuevo Leon, and Chihuahua. As an expat, you should avoid these states if possible, and if it is of utmost importance that you travel to these areas, exercise extreme caution, since the battles between rival cartels or cartels and law enforcement can erupt without any warning and quickly turn violent. Other areas to avoid include the rural areas of northern Sinaloa, Durango, Guerrero, and southern Michoacán. If you happen to travel to these states, always remain within the tourist areas and adhere to local safety advice. Aside from the states mentioned above, the rest of Mexico's 31 states are fairly safe for expats.

In addition, if you don't want to get caught in the drug-related violence, don't go looking for trouble, keep your wits around you and avoid anything to do with the drug trade. Sometimes, even something as going in search for harmless recreational drugs can get you associated with the wrong people, so avoid it as much as possible.

In a few cases, some innocent tourists and expats have found themselves becoming victims of drug-related violence, but these are usually cases of being in the wrong place at the wrong time, and thankfully, there have been very few such cases. This is something that happens even in other countries, not just Mexico, and should therefore not be a major cause for concern.

General Crime In Mexico

Apart from drug-related crime and violence, there are instances of general street crime in some of Mexico's cities, and especially Mexico City, Mexico's capital and its biggest city. However, these are the same kinds of petty street crimes you would expect in other big cities, and the best way to protect yourself is to use common sense. Dress casually, keep your money, expensive gadgets ,and expensive jewelry out of sight, keep a close eye on your belongings and documents, and avoid backstreet alleys and areas without a lot of people, especially at night.

Aside from petty street crime, one form of general crime that is a real issue in Mexico is express kidnappings. This is where criminals kidnap people for a period of 24 to 48 hours while they visit ATMs within the city with your cards and withdraw as much money from your bank account as they can. In most cases, the victim is released after his or her bank accounts have been emptied. The criminals will rarely hurt the victim unless you try to resist or fail to cooperate with their demands. To reduce the risk of being a victim of express kidnappings, avoid using street-side ATMs or ATMs in poorly lit areas or areas with low foot traffic. Opt for ATMs located within banking lobbies and huge malls.

Safety When Using Public Transport

Foreigners should be very alert when using public transportation in Mexico. Some buses are vulnerable to hijackings and theft at night, therefore I'd recommend traveling by bus only during the day. If you are traveling between cities, opt for 'executive, first-class buses' and confirm with the bus that they will use toll roads (locally referred to as *cuotas)* rather than free roads (locally referred to as *libre)*. Crimes are more likely to occur on buses that are traveling on the *libre* roads.

When it comes to using taxis, avoid hailing a taxi off the street. Instead, ask the airport or hotel to hail an official and authorized a taxi for you. While taxis are among the safest ways of getting around in most cities across the world, the situation is different in Mexico. Unregulated street taxis are commonly used as a way of executing express kidnappings and should, therefore, be avoided. Finally, when using the metro in cities like Mexico City and Guadalajara, you should watch out for pickpockets.

Road Safety In Mexico

If you are driving by yourself, you should also be very vigilant and exercise extreme caution. This is because hijackings are also rife on Mexican roads. Avoid driving at night, especially out in the countryside, and if possible, avoid the highways in the areas to the north of the country where drug cartels operate freely, such as the highways between Monterrey, Reynosa, and Nuevo Laredo. Only use toll roads and try as much as possible to avoid free roads. You should also be vigilant when stopping at traffic lights and give yourself ample space to avoid being boxed in. Camper vans and SUVs are the most common targets for carjacking, so avoid them if possible.

So, Is Mexico Safe?

While we have seen that there are indeed high levels of drug-related violence in Mexico, as well as general street crime, the good thing is that the drug-related violence is only concentrated in specific areas of the country, while the general street crime is the same as you would expect in other cities. If you avoid the areas associated with the drug trade, keep your wits around you and settle in areas that are popular with expats, you are unlikely to experience any security-related incidents. If anything, some areas of the country, such as the states of Yucatan, Quintana Roo, and Campeche are even safer than some cities back in the United States. The touristy and expat areas of states like Baja California, Nayarit, Jalisco, and Colima are also fairly safe.

Chapter Eight: Public Transport, Education And Healthcare In Mexico

When you move to Mexico, you will probably not bring your car with you, so you might be curious about how to get around your city and the country. If you are moving with your family, you might also be wondering about schooling for your kids. Finally, your health insurance from back home won't work in Mexico, so you might also want to know about the state of healthcare in the country. In this chapter, we are going to take a look at these three topics–public transport, education, and healthcare.

Public Transport In Mexico

Mexico is a vast country, and unless you only plan to remain holed in your little expat haven for the entirety of your stay in Mexico, it is important to understand how to get around in the country. Fortunately, Mexico has an extensive and well-connected network of transport systems, with a wide range of options to help people get around cities and the country. In addition, one of the many things you will love about Mexico is that public transport in the country is fairly efficient and affordable. With the exception of car rentals, moving around Mexico is very inexpensive.

Before we get into the different modes of transportation available in Mexico, I want to mention one thing – the importance of speaking Spanish. If you intend to get around the country using public transport, and especially using buses, the metro or taxis, you will need to know some Spanish. This is especially important if you will be venturing away from the touristy areas and the big cities. Without some knowledge of Spanish, using public transport might be a bit daunting, therefore I advise that you start learning a few Spanish words.

With that out of the way, let's take a look at some options you have when it comes to getting around the country.

Air Travel

Like I mentioned earlier, Mexico is quite a big country, covering almost two million square kilometers of land. Considering its big size, flying is the fastest and most convenient way of traveling between different parts of the country, especially when you intend to cover long distances. Fortunately, Mexico has an extensive network of modern airports, as well as an ample choice of domestic airlines, including some that offer great service at very competitive prices. This means that you will enjoy a lot of flexibility when it comes to air travel. Mexico also recently signed "Open Skies" agreements with the United States, opening up new routes between Mexican and US cities, giving passengers even more flexibility when it comes to air travel.

Bus

This is another efficient way of traveling across the country, though it is obviously slower than flying. Starting in the early 1990s, the country has made heavy investments in road infrastructure, and as a result, all the country's principal cities and towns are well connected by an extensive network of high-quality roads and highways, with even more roads being added each year to make even the remotest parts of the country accessible.

The availability of an extensive road and highway network has led to the rise of an equally extensive network of professionally run and managed bus service, with buses ranging from modern luxury coaches to more basic buses, some of which are retired school buses that have been converted into public service vehicles. Most Mexican national buses usually provide three classes of service on popular routes. Even the less popular routes will have at least two classes of service. If you are traveling across a long distance, I recommend going to the executive class. Even if it is more expensive, the extra comfort makes up for the cost. Traveling by bus on the executive class is almost comparable to using the National Express in the UK or Greyhound in the United States. Buying bus tickets is pretty easy and is usually done on the spot. However, you might need to book your bus ticket in advance if you are traveling during the high season, such as during the holidays.

Aside from the national buses, there are also local buses that help people move around cities and areas within proximity of the cities. Unlike national buses, there is not much regulation when it comes to local buses. There are no signs restricting the number of passengers on these buses, and sometimes, especially during rush hour, they will carry as many people as can fit inside the bus. Sometimes, you might even see people hanging out the doors during rush hour. Don't be surprised, this is quite normal in Mexico.

These local buses are quite cheap and are usually paid for in cash after boarding. They don't usually issue tickets. While they are not for the faint-hearted, they are a good way to get around cities and towns during the day (especially during the off-peak hours) and are a great way to get to experience Mexico from a local's perspective. When using local buses, it is advisable to dress casually and avoid carrying too much cash or wearing lots of expensive jewelry. Oh and be wary of pickpockets.

Private Car

If you want the convenience of setting your own schedule and traveling without the dependence on public transport, renting a car (or driving your own car) is a great option. If you are contemplating renting a car, you should keep in mind that renting a car in Mexico is more costly than back in the United States. It is almost comparable to renting a car in Europe. You should also remember that the traffic rules in Mexico might be different from what you are used to back at home. If you are driving your own car, don't forget to buy Mexican car insurance.

Driving in Mexico can be a great thing or a very frustrating experience, depending on your location, the time of day, and even the date of the month. In the large cities such as Mexico City, as well as in the highways connecting Mexico City to Puebla, Cuernavaca, and Queretaro, traffic can get very congested, making driving in these areas a very frustrating affair. The experience is even worse during public holidays. On the other hand, driving out in the open road can be a real delight, and is a great way to see the country, especially in places that are not well connected to public transport.

Taxi

Taxis provide another efficient and convenient way of getting around in Mexico. The taxis are also fairly inexpensive compared to what you might be accustomed to back home. Some taxis are metered, which means they charge a standard rate based on time and distance, while others are not metered. For the non-metered taxi, it is at the discretion of the driver to charge you what they feel is a fair rate (ask for the fare amount in advance), and you are free to negotiate with the driver if you feel like you are being overcharged. Like I mentioned earlier, when using a taxi in Mexico, only go for an authorized taxi.

Avoid hailing a taxi on the street, since you could be placing yourself at risk.

Uber

Calling an Uber is another great way of getting around in various parts of the country, and you will love the fact that Uber is a lot cheaper in Mexico compared to the US or the UK. Like in other places, the price of your Uber will sometimes vary based on factors such as the number of Ubers within the area, traffic, as well as the demand for Ubers at that particular moment. Getting around with Uber is pretty safe, and the drivers are helpful and polite. Note that some of them might not understand English, though it is still possible to use an Uber even if you don't understand Spanish. You also have the option of paying for your Uber using cash, as well as credit card and PayPal.

Some cities and towns in Mexico that are served by Uber include Mexico City, Guadalajara, Merida (not at the airport though), Monterrey, Puerto Vallarta, Los Cabos, La Paz (not at the airport), Queretaro, and Toluca. Aside from Uber, there are other ride-hailing services in Mexico. These include Cabify, which is a bit more costly than Uber but has nicer cars, Beat, and Didi Rider, which offers users the cheapest rides.

Train

While Mexico has an extensive railway network, the passenger train service is not active in most of Mexico, after being discontinued in 1997. However, people seeking a thrilling experience can still ride the country's most famous train, which runs on the Copper Canyon Railway. Locals affectionately refer to this famous train *"El Chepe."* In addition, there is another tourist train known as the Tequila

Express, which connects the town of Tequila to Guadalajara. All is not lost, however. There are plans by the Mexican government to reintroduce the passenger train service.

Metro

There is a metro system in the three biggest cities in Mexico–Mexico City, Guadalajara, and Monterrey. If you are in one of these cities, and especially Mexico City, the metro is one of the most convenient ways of getting around the city. The metro system in Mexico City is actually one of the largest in the whole of North America, second only to that in New York. Actually, the city has three metro systems–two that are based on the rail while one is actually a bus.

The main rail-based metro in Mexico is referred to as the El Metro. In most places, it runs underneath the city, though there are some few stretches where it runs above ground as well. The El Metro is used by more than four and a half million people every day. The El Metro consists of 12 lines that connect most areas of the city to the city center. The other rail-based metro system is the Tren Ligero (Spanish for a light train), which serves the southern areas of Mexico City.

Finally, there is the Metro Bus service, which began operation in 2006. It runs on a dedicated bus lane along the 35 miles long Avenida Insurgentes–the world's longest commercial boulevard. The outer lane on each side of the Avenida Insurgentes is used exclusively by Metrobus, with stations at several points along the avenue. The Metrobus is also a very efficient way of getting around Mexico City, though the buses get very congested at times. However, the Metrobus has been so successful in Mexico City that it has also been replicated in cities like Acapulco.

Paying for your Metro ride in Mexico City is quite easy. If you are using the El Metro, you can use a Metro Card or purchase small cardboard tickets using cash. The tickets will get you through the turnstiles. For the Tren Ligero and the Metrobus, you will need the Metro Card. The card can be topped up with cash at the ticket counter, or with credit at machines.

Colectivo

A collective is basically a shared taxi operating within a specific route. Colectivos can be a van, a car, or even a pickup truck carrying passengers headed in the same direction. Colectivos will pick and drop passengers anywhere along the route. Just like the local buses, colectivos are unregulated, which means that they will try to carry as many passengers as can fit into the vehicle.

Mototaxi

Mototaxis are three-wheeled vehicles with a bench seat at the back. They are usually referred to as tuk-tuks or rickshaws in most parts of the world. You will mostly find these on the outskirts of big cities and within smaller towns. They are a very cheap way of getting around, though they might not take you outside of their restricted zones.

As you can see, there is no shortage of public transport options to help you get around Mexico, whether you want to travel within the city or town or between different cities across the country.

Education

If you have a young family, one of your considerations, as you prepare for the move to Mexico, will be whether you will be able to get a high-quality education for your children. In the past, the Mexican education system wasn't the best, but there have been improvements in the recent past, and any expats moving to Mexico with their family now have a couple of options when it comes to their children's education. Currently, the education system in Mexico is under the regulation of the *Secretaría de Educación Pública*, which has ensured that public schools are now well-funded (at least in the urban areas) and made education compulsory for children until the age of eighteen.

The Mexican Education System

Education in Mexico starts with pre-school, which is open for kids from the age of three. Pre-school is privately funded. In the past, it was not mandatory for kids to attend preschool, but the *Secretaría de Educación Pública* made it mandatory beginning in 2018. After pre-school, children join a primary school (*primaria*), which runs from grades one to six and is mandatory for children aged six to twelve. Primary school is funded by the government.

After primary school, children between the ages of twelve to sixteen advance to middle school or junior high school (referred to as *Secundaria* in Mexico). The middle school covers grades seven to nine and is also compulsory. Middle school is also funded by the government, which means kids learn free of charge.

After middle school, students between the ages of fifteen to eighteen advance to high school or preparatory school (referred to as *Preparatoria* in Mexico), which covers grades ten to twelve. High school education is also funded by the government and is the last phase of education that is mandatory.

Once they have cleared high school, students can now advance to University, though a high percentage do not, especially in the rural areas of the country. Mexican University education is similar to that in the US. Students will complete their undergraduate bachelor's degree (*Licenciatura*) in four years, the Master's degree (*Maestria*) in two years, while a Doctoral degree (*Doctorado*) will take three years. For students who do opt not to go to university, they have the option of undertaking commercial or technology programs that will help them prepare for a productive future without pursuing higher education.

As an expat, sending your children exclusively to a public school is not the best option because of two reasons. First, most public schools are only taught in Spanish, which means that your children might miss out on some things unless they are bilingual. In addition, some public schools are under-funded, while some are even rife with corruption.

What many expats do is to send their children to public schools for half a day and then have the children home-schooled for the other half of the day. Having your children attend Mexican public schools is a great way to get your kids to learn Spanish and integrate well into the local culture. Alternatively, you could send your children to a private school. Private schools are better funded and have better bilingual integration.

Before sending your child to a private school, confirm that the school has received accreditation from the Ministry of Public Education. Quality also varies from one private school to another, so it is advisable to visit the school, check its curriculum and meet with the teachers to ascertain the quality of the school. If you intend to have your children pursue higher education back in your home country, you should also confirm whether the private school has international accreditation.

Healthcare

Health is a very critical issue, and before moving and settling in a foreign country, it is good to be aware of the level of healthcare you can expect in the country. Fortunately, Mexico has a high standard of healthcare that you will also find to be quite inexpensive compared to your home country. The healthcare system in Mexico comprises three levels.

Seguro Popular

This is the first level of healthcare in Mexico. It is a form of public healthcare that is reserved for Mexican citizens without formal employment. Expatriates who have earned residency status (both temporary and permanent) may also qualify for Seguro Popular. However, since this is reserved for people who are not covered by IMSS (the second level) and cannot afford private health insurance, you will need to prove that you have very low income. If you are covered by the Seguro Popular, you can get treated at one of the Seguro medical centers free of charge.

The IMSS

This is the second level of healthcare in Mexico, which is operated by the Mexican Social Security Institute (referred to as the *Instituto Mexicano del Seguro Social* or IMSS in Mexico). This program is open to citizens and expatriates working under the private sector. This program is funded by the federal government, the private employer and the employee. Part of the employee's salary is deducted to pay for the program, while the employer matches with an equal amount. It is also possible for retired expats to join the IMSS program, though you will need to make a monthly contribution to the program.

Private Healthcare

While public healthcare in Mexico is of high quality, a high number of expats prefer private healthcare because it offers the highest quality of medical care. However, private hospitals are way more expensive than public hospitals, even though they might still come across as cheap when compared to your home country. Many of them will require you to provide insurance information or pay a deposit in advance before getting treatment. Many of the doctors working in the private sector undertake their medical training either in the USA or in Europe, therefore many of them are fluent in English, and the level of medical care they provide is at par with what you would receive back at home. If you are already covered by the IMSS but would still like to be treated at a private hospital, you will need to have additional health insurance or pay for the extra expenses from your own pocket.

Getting Health Insurance In Mexico

Most expats who opt for treatment in private hospitals usually pay for their minor bills from their pocket, while reserving private health insurance for emergency cases. When it comes to private health insurance for in Mexico, there are two major plans. The first one is the national plan which is sold by local companies and will keep you covered as long as you are in Mexico. The other is the international plan which is sold by international insurance companies (most of them from the US) and keeps you covered all over the world. It is also good to note that there are some Mexican private hospitals that accept insurance from foreign countries. If you happen to be near such a hospital, you can still maintain the insurance cover you had back at home.

It's good to note that most private insurance plans in Mexico will not cover pre-existing medical conditions, while others will charge you a higher deductible to cover any pre-existing conditions. Sometimes, filing claims can also be a bit hectic, therefore it is best to have a broker to represent you and help you with filing the claims.

Instead of getting private health insurance in Mexico, some expats from the US also choose to maintain their Medicare. In case they need some treatment that they cannot cover for out-of-pocket, they fly back home to receive treatment that will be covered by Medicare. For this to work, you will need to continue paying for Medicare even while you are living in Mexico. This is especially a good option for those who are not moving to Mexico permanently and might back to the US later.

Dental Care In Mexico

Receiving dental care in Mexico is a very easy and pretty straightforward affair. Just walk into the dentist's office, explain your problem to the dentist, have your tooth filled or removed or whatever else is required, pay in cash and leave. That's it. You don't have to deal with countless forms or advance appointments or worry about being passed off to the dentist's assistant. What's more, the service is of very high quality, despite being very affordable. Considering how affordable dental care is in Mexico, most expats pay for it out of their own pockets, without involving their insurance company.

It's also important to note that the price of dental care in Mexico will vary depending on the area. Dentists working in expat and tourist towns are generally more expensive because they know they can charge more for their expat or tourist clients while still remaining way cheaper compared to dentists back in the US, Canada or Europe. At the same time, just because they charge higher doesn't mean that the quality of service is any better than is offered by dentists serving the local community in private hospitals. Therefore, it is far much better to visit dentists serving the local community. With such dentists, you can expect to pay only about 10 or 20 percent of what you would have paid for dental care back at home. Dentists that cater predominantly to tourists and expats will charge you about 40 to 50 percent of what you would have paid back home.

Chapter Nine: Working In Mexico

Majority of foreigners who make a permanent move are usually retirees looking to spend their golden years enjoying Mexico's warm weather and laid-back lifestyle. However, in the last couple of years, there has been a growing number of working-age professionals looking to move to and work in Mexico. This has been spurred by Mexico's rapidly growing economy, a booming engineering and architecture industry, and of course, the lower costs of living in the country. If you are one of the young professionals looking to move and settle in Mexico, this chapter will tell you everything you need to know about working in Mexico.

Before we get started, I want to give a disclaimer. While a high number of people in Mexico understand English, especially in the big cities, having a passable knowledge of Spanish will increase your chances of getting a job. With that out of the way, let's jump in.

Can Foreigners Legally Work In Mexico?

It is perfectly legal for foreigners to work in Mexico, provided they have been granted the "permission to work" visa. In order to receive the "permission to work" visa, you will need to meet one of the following conditions:

- You should have already received a job offer from a Mexican company
- Your application should be sponsored by a foreign company with subsidiaries or operations in Mexico.
- You should have some special skills that are needed in the country

You can also come to Mexico and work legally if you are working for a foreign company, provided the remuneration for your work comes from abroad, rather from a Mexican company or a company with subsidiaries in Mexico.

You can also be granted a work permit in Mexico by showing that it is your intention to invest in the country. For instance by setting up a company within the country, or investing in the Mexican Stock Exchange. In order to attain a work permit through this route, you will need to make an investment that is equivalent to 40,000 times Mexico's daily minimum salary. Note that this multiple might change at any time without prior notice.

These stipulations are put in place to ensure that foreigners do not end up taking jobs that could have been done by Mexican citizens and to ensure that foreigners coming into the country will be able to support themselves without having to rely on the Mexican state.

What Kind of Work Can You Do In Mexico?

Foreigners moving to Mexico have a number of options when it comes to working in Mexico. The kind of work that is most suitable for you will be dependent on your circumstances. Some types of work you can engage in as a foreigner in Mexico include:

Corporate Work: This is where a foreigner is employed either by a Mexican company or by a multinational company with operations within Mexico. In most cases, you will need some specialist knowledge or skills in order to be eligible for corporate work in Mexico. If you are coming to Mexico for corporate work, the logistics of your move into the country and the requisite legal paperwork will typically be handled by the company you are coming to work for. If you want to move to Mexico for corporate work, you are more likely to get a job in Mexico if your skills are based on industries where Mexico typically has to seek help from outside. These include industries like IT, Medicine, Science, and Teaching, especially at the higher education level.

Freelancing: A high number of young foreigners who are moving into the country are freelancers working in the knowledge economy, such as photographers, consultants, writers and journalists, graphic designers, translators, web developers, and so on. Many of these freelancers perform their work remotely and have contracts with clients abroad, only using Mexico as a base from where they work. Such work arrangements have been made possible by the internet and modern communication technologies. Since their remuneration does not come from Mexico (for most of them at least), such freelancers do not need a "permission to work" visa in order to work in the country. This working model is very advantageous since most of these freelancers enjoy the benefits of living in a country with a low cost of living while earning their income in stronger currencies, such as dollars and euros.

Self-employment: As a foreigner, you could also set up your small business in Mexico. Some of the most popular small businesses among foreigners include hotels, restaurants and bars, relocation services and real estate. An increasing number of foreigners are also setting up small businesses selling consultancy services, especially in the fields of IT and business development. If you intend to start such a small business, it is important to ensure that you have enough capital to keep the business running before it becomes well-established enough to sustain itself.

Teaching English: Teaching English as a second language or a foreign language is one of the most popular jobs among foreigners living in Mexico. There are also lots of such jobs, which can be found through one of the many job boards in the country. There is a lot of demand for English teachers because Mexicans who want to receive professional qualification will usually need to learn English. Before getting a job as an English teacher, you will need to hold the TEFL certification.

Volunteering: It is also possible to find work in Mexico as a volunteer, taking part in social and community projects and helping local communities by sharing your experience and knowledge. Some of the most popular fields for foreign volunteers in Mexico include social programs, environmental programs, wildlife conservation, and marine conservation, and especially the conservation of sea turtles. Since volunteer work is unremunerated, you won't need a permit to perform this kind of work.

Casual work: Casual work essentially means working in the country without proper permissions, or in other words, illegally. This can either take the form of getting employment on a cash-in-hand basis or setting up casual businesses, such as a small store or a stall at the local market. However, I do not recommend this route. First, if you get employment on a cash-in-hand basis, you will find that the pay is very poor, owing to Mexico's low minimum hourly wages. On the other hand, immigration officers routinely conduct spot-checks to find any foreigners working on a casual basis or running casual businesses, and therefore, you are unlikely to work for long without being detected. If you are found to be working in the country illegally, you can expect to be deported.

Getting A Job In Mexico

There is a high rate of unemployment in Mexico, and therefore, finding a job in the country might be a bit harder compared to finding one in your home country. If you plan on moving to and working in Mexico (corporate work), you should start your job search early. The most convenient way of finding a job in Mexico is to use the internet– check job forums and websites, as well as the websites of companies you might be interested in working for. Alternatively, if you are already in Mexico, you can check for job openings in local newspapers or sign up with a recruitment agency. If you have friends already working in Mexico, you can also reach out to them and let them know that you are looking for a job, since word of mouth is still pretty effective in Mexico.

Working Hours

In most Mexican places, the workday is similar to that of the UK. Work usually starts at 8.00 in the morning. Employees are allowed a one hour break for lunch and can leave work anywhere between 5.00 and 7.00 in the evening. Some companies may have a longer lunch break (Descanso) lasting between 1.00 and 4.00 pm, in accordance with the traditional Mexican working hours. For such companies, employees will usually start leaving the office at 6.00 in the evening.

While finding employment in Mexico might be a little more challenging than in your home country, there are still a high number of foreigners who are living and working in Mexico, and with some little forward planning, you can also find work and live a comfortable life in Mexico. Living and working in Mexico is especially easy for foreigners who engage in freelance work, working remotely with clients outside Mexico.

Chapter Ten: Paying Taxes In Mexico

As an expat living in Mexico, whether you are a resident or not, you will be required to pay taxes if you earn any kind of income, whether that is from a job, from a business, from your investments and interest-bearing bank accounts in Mexico, or from your properties. Even if you don't have an income, you will still pay sales tax (VAT) on most of the goods and services you procure while in the country. In this chapter, I am going to give you an overview of the Mexican tax system to give you a general idea of what taxes you might be expected to pay. However, if you are earning an income in the country, I would recommend talking to a professional tax specialist to ensure you are in compliance with all the tax requirements that apply to you.

Who Is Required To Pay Income Tax In Mexico

The taxes you will be required to pay as a foreigner living in Mexico will depend on your tax status. There are two basic classifications of tax status:

• **Resident taxpayer**: In Mexico, you will be classified as a resident for tax purposes based on the length of time you have stayed in the country. Aside from looking at your official residency status, there are other considerations that will be taken into account to determine whether you fit under the resident classification for tax purposes.

If the Servicio de Administración Tributaria (SAT)–Mexico's tax administration body – believes that your "center of vital interests" lies within the country, then you will be classified as a resident taxpayer. Your "center of vital interests" is considered if you either earn at least half of your income within the country, have a home in the country, or if your main professional interests are carried out within Mexico.

If you are classified as a resident taxpayer, the Mexican authorities will expect you to pay taxes on any income you make within and outside Mexico.

• **Non-resident taxpayer:** If your "center of vital interests" does not lie within the country, you will be classified as a non-resident taxpayer. In this case, you will only be required to pay taxes on the income that is earned within the country.

Income Tax in Mexico

You will be required to pay income tax to Mexican authorities if you are employed, own properties that you are renting out, own a business, or have interest-bearing securities or bank accounts within the country. Basically, if you earn any form of income within the country, you will be required to file tax returns in Mexico. Additionally, if you are a resident taxpayer as we saw above, you will also be required to file taxes for income earned even outside the country.

The amount of income tax you are required to pay in Mexico will vary based on how much you earn, any deductions that you are eligible for, and other factors. Generally, the income tax rates for residents will range from 1.92% to 35%, while the rates for non-residents will range between 15% and 30%. Companies in Mexico are required to pay 30% tax.

If your only source of income is employment by a Mexico based employer, the employer will typically withhold your tax and remit it to the government through a pay as you earn model. In this case, all you will need to do is file your tax declaration, without having to pay anything since your employer will already have submitted your tax payments. The tax year in Mexico runs from 1st January to 31st December, and the tax returns for the previous year should be filed by the 30th of April. Tax returns are usually filed online.

Property Tax In Mexico

If you own property in Mexico, you will also need to pay taxes for the property. Fortunately, property taxes in Mexico are significantly lower when compared to countries such as the United States and Canada. There are three types of taxes associated with owning property in Mexico. These are:

- **Acquisition tax**: This is the initial tax that is paid at the time of purchasing the property. Acquisition tax is usually charged at 2% of the cost of purchasing the property. It is usually paid in cash to the local municipality, though some small percentage might also go to the state in some cases.
- **Annual property tax**: This is a tax that is paid every year to the municipality in which the property lies. Payments are usually made in cash at the municipal office. It is advisable to pay the annual property tax in January since you might get early payment discounts. An average home in Mexico will only cost you a few hundred dollars in annual property tax, though the rate will vary between different municipalities and states. If your property is in a rural area, you might even find yourself paying less than $100 in annual property taxes.
- **Capital Gains Tax:** If you decide to sell your property, you will need to pay Capital Gains tax, which is locally referred to as *Impuesto Sobre la Renta* (ISR). There are two ways of calculating capital gains tax. The first option is to pay 20% of the value of the transaction. Alternatively, you could pay between 28% and 30% of the net gain minus expenses such as commissions, improvements, and other expenses. You are allowed to use whatever option you feel is most favorable to you. It is advisable to have a notary help you with paying capital gains tax.

Sales Tax

In Mexico, retail goods and services are charged a sales tax – Value Added Tax (VAT) or *Impuesto al Valor Agregado* (IVA) in Spanish. In most cases, the sales tax is included in the price of the good or service, though some establishments, especially in areas that are popular with tourists, it is separate from the price of the item. Currently, the IVA stands at 16% in most of the country. In the border regions, the IVA stands at 11% of the price of the item.

Tax Exemptions In Mexico

Depending on your specific situation, it is possible to be eligible for some deductions from your gross income that help reduce your taxable income. However, there is a cap on the deductions, which generally stands at 15%. This means that your deductions will not exceed 15% of your gross income, even if your expenses are eligible for deductions. Still, there are some exceptions to this rule. Some deductions you might be eligible for will fall into one of the following categories:

Personal deductible items: Expenses covering things such as medical and dental bills, education, as well as charity donations are eligible for deduction from your taxable income. Personal deductions are capped at 15%. However, there are some exceptions. For instance, you are allowed to exceed the limit for medical expenses, though you will have to present a medical certificate from a government hospital to be allowed to make deductions exceeding this limit. On the other hand, deductions for charity donations are capped at 7%, rather than 15%.

Business deductible items: For self-employed expats, some business expenses might be eligible for deductions before you calculate your tax due. However, this is a pretty complicated issue, and it is best to seek the services of a professional tax accountant to make sure you have everything in order.

Are You Required To Pay Tax Back At Home?

Many foreigners living and working in Mexico and paying their taxes to Mexican authorities are worried that they might still be required to pay taxes back in their home country, which would amount to double taxation. Fortunately, Mexico has a reciprocal tax agreement with most countries, which in effect means that foreigners working in Mexico and paying their taxes in Mexico are not required to pay taxes back at home.

If you are from the US, however, the situation is a little different. The United States and Ethiopia are the two countries in the world that require all their citizens to file their taxes at home, regardless of where they are living or working. Therefore, if you are from the US, you will need to declare foreign earned income. However, if your foreign earnings do not exceed $102,100, the earnings will not be taxed, though you will still have to declare the earnings.

With the information provided in this chapter, you now have a working understanding of the tax system in Mexico and what is required of you as an expat working in Mexico. However, taxation can be a complicated topic, and therefore, I recommend seeking the advice of a professional tax accountant to make sure that you are in compliance with all the tax requirements.

Chapter Eleven: Moving Your Things To Mexico

For most people, moving has never been an easy thing. Even moving from one area of the city to another, or from one city to the next often comes with its fair share of challenges. When it comes to moving, not to a new neighborhood or the next city, but a different country, then it becomes a whole different ball game. Not only do you have to deal with the ordinary aspects of moving, like deciding what to carry and what not to, packing and finding movers, but you also have to worry about whether your items will be allowed in the new country, getting the appropriate documentation for the items, getting them insured and arranging international insurance, and so on.

The good thing about moving to Mexico is that the Mexican government has no qualms about people moving and settling in Mexico, and therefore, they allow people moving into Mexico to bring their household possessions into the country duty-free. However, it's not as easy as loading your belongings into a truck and heading south. In this chapter, we are going to look at the most important things you need to know concerning moving your things into Mexico, including how your immigration status affects your move, what documents are required, what things you are allowed to bring into the country and what things are not allowed, moving with pets, and so on.

Immigration Status

In order to be allowed to bring your household goods into Mexico, you need to have applied for and been granted either temporary or permanent residency in the country. If you are coming into the country with a tourist visa, you won't be allowed to bring your household goods into the country. This means that, if your plan is to settle in the country with only the tourist visa and make border runs every six months to renew your tourist visa, you will have to purchase all the household goods you need in Mexico. Fortunately, a lot of rental houses in Mexico are fully furnished, therefore you might not need to buy a lot of stuff.

Foreigners can import their household goods in one of two ways, depending on their immigration status.

Temporary Import: This is for foreigners coming into Mexico under the temporary residency visa. Technically, the temporary visa means that they will have to return to their home country at some point (unless they acquire a permanent residency visa), and therefore, their household goods are also imported into Mexico on a temporary basis. Under the temporary import permit, the foreigners will be required to carry back their household goods with them to their home country. They are not allowed to give the items away or sell them in Mexico. In case one acquires permanent residence, they will also need to apply for a permanent import status for their household goods.

Permanent Import: This is for foreigners coming into Mexico under a permanent residency visa, as well as Mexican citizens returning into the country after living abroad for a period exceeding two years. Since they are moving into the country indefinitely, they are under no legal requirement to return the goods to their home country.

It is good to note that you required to import your household goods duty-free into Mexico either three months before you arrive in the country or six months after you arrive. In addition, you are only allowed to import your household goods duty-free into the country once in a lifetime, therefore you should put enough consideration into what items you carry with you and what items you leave behind.

What Documents Do You Need To Import Household Goods Into Mexico?

Below is a list of the main documents you will require in order to be allowed to import your household goods into the country. Sometimes, you might be asked for additional documentation, depending on your circumstances.

- Your resident card – Remember, you need to have residency status to be allowed to import household goods into the country. The visa stickers issued by the consulate in your home country will not work.
- Airway bill (AWB) – required if you are shipping your household goods by air. If you are shipping them by sea, you will need to provide the bill of lading (BOL).
- Packing list – this is a list cataloguing all your goods, and will include details such as your name, origin address, address where the goods are headed, a shipping box number for each box, a description of all the items in each box, total weight of each box, total number of boxes, and the declared value of the items.
- Proof of the last date of entry – Such as a reservation or an airline ticket.
- Proof of address – A document, such as a utility bill, to confirm your address, dated not more than three months from your last date of entry.
- Your passport
- Letter of declaration – This will include a description of the goods, your address in Mexico, and an acknowledgment that you are under obligation to take your goods with you when you return to your home country (for temporary imports) and that you are under obligation to notify customs authorities in case your Mexican address changes.
- Letter of empowerment – this gives your customs broker authority to transport and handle your goods.

- Declaration of household goods – this is usually necessary for permanent imports. It is optional for temporary imports, though it might become necessary sometimes, especially when you are importing a lot of goods.

What Goods Qualify As Household Goods?

The only items that foreigners are allowed to import into the country duty-free are household goods and personal effects. These are items such as furniture, clothes, electronics and appliances, books, decorations, and any other items that are normally part of the household. The amount should not exceed the quantities that are ordinarily used in a normal house. Personal medical equipment, such as oxygen generators, sugar and blood pressure monitors, wheelchairs, and so on can also be brought into the country duty-free. The same applies to tools that are necessary either for your profession or your hobbies. In order for these items to be allowed into the country duty-free, they must be used. If they are new or look new, you will be required to pay duty for them and adhere to other importation restrictions. Therefore, if you buy some items just before your move, this will make moving more expensive.

What Are You Not Allowed To Bring Into Mexico?

There are also some restrictions on what you cannot bring with you into the country. You are not allowed to bring things such as spices, foods, both fresh and frozen, seeds, or plants. It is illegal to bring drugs into the country, even if they are legal in your home country. If you are on medication, you should carry the medication as part of your luggage, rather than shipping it with your household items. It is also recommended that you have a copy of your prescription as a precaution. Don't ship items such as expensive perfumes and cosmetics. Toiletries, detergents, and car cleaning chemicals should not be shipped. If you plan to bring vehicles into the country, you should note that these do not qualify as household goods and will, therefore, need to go through a different process. Finally, you are not allowed to bring ammunition, guns, or other weapons into the country.

Can You Bring Your Pets Into The Country?

There is no problem with bringing your pets into the country, and you have the option of either having them enter into the country with you as passenger luggage or shipping them together with your household items. You are allowed to bring up to 3 animals into the country duty-free. Before the animals are allowed into the country, you will need to present health certificates for the animals, issued by animal health officers in your country and showing that the animals have received their vaccinations. If you decide to ship your pets as living cargo, note that there might be some extra shipping charges. Some airlines might also not allow pets to be carried as luggage, so it is important to confirm this before booking your tickets.

At the point of entry, the animals will also be inspected to confirm that they do not have any diseases that are transferable to humans. Any animals that look ill will have to be further examined by a licensed health officer. If your puppy is less than 4 months old and has therefore not been vaccinated, you will be required to keep it confined until it is old enough to be vaccinated, and for an extra 30 days after getting the shots.

Can You Bring Your Car Into The Country?

I mentioned earlier that cars, motorcycles, and other vehicles do not qualify as household goods and will, therefore, have to be imported separately. Below are some guidelines regarding the importation of cars into the country:

Temporary Importation Of Cars

If you are coming into the country on a tourist visa or a temporary residence visa, you are allowed to bring your car (with foreign plates) into the country as a temporary import. You will only be allowed to bring one car into the country. If you intend to drive the car beyond the "free zone," which extends up to 35 km from the border, you will have to apply for a Temporary Import Permit (TIP). These are only available at the border crossing points and should be gotten before crossing into the country. However, you can drive a foreign-plated vehicle in the States of Baja California and Sonora without a TIP.

If you are coming into the country using a tourist visa, the TIP will remain valid for a period of 180 days, after which you will have to leave the country and receive another permit upon re-entry, which will be valid for another 180 days. You can come back with the same car or a separate car. However, you cannot bring another car into the country if the previous one has not left the country. If you came into the country under a temporary residency visa, your TIP will remain valid for as long as your temporary residency visa remains valid. Since the vehicle will be in the country as a temporary import, it cannot be issued with Mexican plates, and will, therefore, have to maintain its foreign plates.

It's also good to note that any vehicle that comes into the country as a temporary import must return to its home country. You are not allowed to sell the vehicle in Mexico. In addition, the vehicle can only be driven by your direct family members (whether Mexican citizens or foreigners) and other foreigners. Mexican citizens (who are not your family members) are not allowed to drive such a car unless a foreigner is with them in the car.

Permanent Importation Of Cars

For those coming into the country under a permanent residency visa, you are not allowed to import a vehicle with foreign plates into the country as a temporary import. Instead, you will have to bring in the vehicle as a permanent import, which means you will have to get it registered with the Mexican authorities. As a permanent resident in Mexico, you are not allowed to drive a car with foreign plates. Getting your vehicle legalized in Mexico is not an easy process, and I recommend selling your car back at home and buying another one in Mexico. If you decide to go through with the process, however, I recommend that you seek the help of a customs agent, because this process can be quite complicated and will vary depending on your type of car, its age, engine size, and so on.

While the law about permanent residents not being allowed to drive vehicles with foreign plates is not strictly enforced, if you encounter the Federales, the vehicle will be confiscated and impounded.

As you can see, moving your things into Mexico is not a very complicated process. If you find yourself having any questions or doubts about bringing something into the country, however, it is best to seek the advice of a customs agent so that you don't end up on the wrong side of the law or facing hefty fines.

Chapter Twelve: Cultural Shock
When Moving To Mexico

Mexico may be a next-door neighbor to the United States, but when it comes to culture, they might as well be on opposite sides of the planet. If you have visited Mexico for a short time as a tourist, you might not have experienced many of the differences, especially if you stuck to the areas that are frequented by tourists. Once you start your life there, however, that's when the differences will become apparent, and it is inevitable that you will experience some culture shock, at least during your first couple of months in the country.

The language is different, the locals may have some behaviors and characteristics you are not accustomed to, the food might be different from what you are used to, and so on, and sometimes, it is easy to become angry and judgmental over the small things that seem foreign to you. However, letting the practices and nuances of locals get to you will only make your move to the country more frustrating, since you cannot possibly change the behaviors and traits of all the 130 million Mexicans living in the country. And after all, what is the point of moving to another country if you want everything to remain as it is back in your home country?

The key to a great experience following your move to Mexico, or any other country for that matter, is to start learning and understanding the nuances of the local culture. Once you take the time to understand them, they become more tolerable, and the culture shock dissipates much faster. Who knows, you might even start enjoying some little things you found annoying at the start of your stay in the country.

In this chapter, we are going to take a look at some main sources of culture shock for gringos moving and settling in Mexico.

Language Barrier

Spanish is Mexico's de facto official language and is the most widely spoken language in the country, spoken by about 90% of the population as a first language (there are other languages spoken in Mexico, such as Nahuatl, Yucatec Maya ,and Mixtec). While some Mexicans speak English, especially in the tourist-frequented areas and the big cities, the majority do not. As an expat living in Mexico, it is possible to comfortably live with minimal knowledge of Spanish, especially if you stick to the areas with a high expat population, where the majority of people speak and understand English.

However, if you are planning to venture further away from the bigger cities, or if you are looking for employment within the country, it is important to have a passable understanding of Spanish. Knowing the language will also make it easier for you to negotiate for better prices with vendors/landlords, understand local signs and instructions, understand the information on product packaging, and so on.

Therefore, if you want to be able to adapt to life in Mexico much faster, you should commit yourself to learn the local language. What's more, you don't need to get to native-level mastery of language. Just knowing some basic Spanish, enough to help you communicate simply will go a long way in helping you to fit into society and improve your life in the country. In addition, showing the effort to speak in the local language, even with mispronounced words and stutters, will help you create a rapport with locals and place you in better favor with them. They will even be more willing to go out of their way to help you if you show that you appreciate the local language. On the other hand, making no attempt to speak to locals in the local language might even be seen as rude in some areas.

If you are moving to the country and don't speak even the slightest Spanish, it is advisable to learn at least some few phrases to help you create a rapport with the locals from the moment you land.

Below are some common Spanish words and phrases to help you get started.

Hola—This term is a general greeting, similar to saying "hi." Mexicans love greetings, and every time you have to talk to a stranger, start by greeting them. For instance, when you go to talk to the hotel receptionist, or a taxi driver, start by greeting them. Using the term *hola* is fine for informal uses. There are also some greetings that are time sensitive, just like in English. For instance, to say good morning to someone, use the phrase *Buenos Dias*. To say good afternoon to someone, say *Buenas tardes*. To say good evening or good night, use the phrase *Buenas Noches*. If someone calls you on the telephone, you can answer with any of the following phrases: *hola, alo, diga* or *Bueno*. To wish someone goodbye, you can use the following phrases: *adios, hasta la vista,* or *hasta luego*.

Que Onda? – This phrase is an informal way of greeting a friend. It is similar to asking someone "what's up?"

Como Esta Usted? – This is a Spanish phrase that means "how are you?" If you are in an informal conversation, say with a friend, you can shorten the phrase to *Como estas?* If you meet someone and they say these words to you, you should reply with *Bien gracias y usted,* or *Bien gracias y tu?* which are the formal and informal ways of saying "fine, thank you, and how are you?"

Gracias – This means thank you. Mexicans are ordinarily very polite, and you should use this word whenever someone provides you with a service. To say "thank you very much" use the phrase *muchas gracias.*

Cuanto cuesta? – This term is used to ask for the price of something. If you just finished eating at a restaurant, you should say *la cuenta por favor,* which means "bill/check please."

Como se Llama usted? – This phrase means "what is your name?" This is more formal. If you want to ask for someone's name in an informal setting, you should say *Como te Llamas?* If someone asks you one of these questions, you should answer with *Me llamo/Mi nombre es* followed by your name. For instance, if someone asks my name, I will say *Mi nombre es Raul* for formal settings and *Me Llamo Raul* for informal settings. After getting introduced to someone, you can express your pleasure in meeting them with the phrase *Mucho gusto, Encantado.* For women, you should say *encantada* instead of *encantado.*

Hablas Inglés/Español? – If you are not sure whether someone speaks English/Spanish, use this phrase to find out. It basically means "do you speak English/Spanish?" If someone asks you this and you don't speak Spanish, you can answer with *no hablo español.* If you speak a little Spanish, answer with *si, un poco.*

These are a few of the phrases that will come in handy when interacting with locals. It's good to note that the Spanish spoken by locals will sound a little different from the Spanish spoken in Spain, or the Spanish you might have learned in class. This is because Mexicans have their own version of Spanish slang. If you want to learn the local language much faster and start talking like a real Mexican, you can check out my book on Mexican slang, which is aptly titled Mexislang. The book is available on Kindle and Paperback on Amazon and as an audiobook on Audible, and you can get it for free with your Audible free trial.

Aside from a language barrier, another communication barrier is that Mexicans, just like Asians and other Latin Americans, are extremely helpful and polite, and hate to disappoint people. However, this aversion can actually turn into a source of disappointment. For instance, Mexicans will give you assurances that something can be done on time or on a budget, even when they know it's not possible. This will lead to time extensions or increases in the budget later on. If you ask someone for directions, they might give you the wrong directions instead of saying that they don't know. If you invite someone to a social engagement, they will accept the invitation even if they don't plan to attend. They feel that declining the invitation is more disappointing than failing to show up later.

While Mexicans who are used to working with foreigners or those who have lived in the United States do not typically have this problem, it is common amongst most locals, and it is best to be prepared for it, else it can lead to lots of frustrations. You should be very cautious about affirmative responses, especially those that come very quickly and in business matters. If possible, get multiple opinions to make sure someone was not just placating you with an affirmative response.

Time In Mexico

One of the factors that make Mexico an ideal place for vacations and retirement is its significantly laid-back lifestyle. Unlike Americans, Mexicans never seem to be in a rush, and this leisurely pace can be a great thing when you are on vacation. However, if you just moved there from a country like the United States, this leisurely pace can be very frustrating. Tasks that usually got completed back at home will take much longer in Mexico. There will be delays that would have been inexcusable back at home. People do not follow a rigid schedule, especially when it comes to social engagements. For instance, if a friend is hosting a party at 2 o'clock, everyone, including the host and the other guests know that the party will start half an hour to an hour later. Being late to social engagements is not seen as rude in Mexico. To Mexicans, schedules are merely meant as guidelines, not exact rules that need to be followed strictly. However, this does not apply to business meetings, doctor's meetings, travel schedules, and other official situations.

Bureaucracy

Another thing that a lot of foreigners find frustrating about Mexico is the endless paperwork and bureaucratic red tape. Whenever you need to perform any official or legal tasks, from opening bank accounts to renting or buying a property, you will have to file mountains of paperwork and give endless signatures. In addition, most of the paperwork will have to be officially stamped in order to be considered valid. Don't make the mistake of misplacing this paperwork, because you might be required to produce it later on in order to get some other service or to prove something. I know this can be a bit exasperating, but there is not much you can do about it. Even most of us locals are equally fed up with all this bureaucratic red tape.

Mexican Food

It is impossible to talk about Mexico's culture without mentioning Mexican food. When most gringos, especially Americans, hear about Mexican food, they automatically think about tacos and burritos. However, there is more to Mexican food than that. One distinct thing you will notice about Mexican food and cuisine is that it is literally packed with flavor. Spices and herbs such as onions, garlic, cinnamon, oregano, limes and lemons, cocoa, coriander (referred to as cilantro in the US), and a variety of chilies–chipotles, habaneros, serranos, jalapenos, poblanos, and so on–are a major part of Mexican cooking. This is why most foreigners feel like Mexican food is very hot and spicy. Unlike what is a common back in the United States, Mexicans don't typically use cheese in foods like enchiladas and tacos. Even in cases where they do, they prefer Mexican handmade cheese, rather than the cheeses that "Mexican restaurants" back in the US use.

Mexican food varies from region to region, owing to both the climate and geography of the region and the ethnic groups that inhabit the region. For instance, cuisine from Mexico's northern region is defined by beef, goat, and ostrich meat. In the Yucatan peninsula, which is known for a slow-roasted pork dish known as *cochinita pibil,* the foods are less spicy and a bit sweeter. In Oaxaca, one of the regions with some of the best Mexican food, their cuisine is defined by the rich and tasty mole sauces and the savory tamales. The areas around central Mexico are famous for pre-Columbian meat stews known as *pozole* and braised or roasted pork *carnitas.* The regions around southeastern Mexico, on the other hand, are known for their spicy chicken, fish and vegetable dishes with a Caribbean influence. In other words, Mexican cuisine is as diverse as the country itself.

Meals And Mealtimes In Mexico

Just as the food in Mexico is different from what you might be used to back at home, so are the mealtimes in Mexico. I often see tourists walking into Mexican restaurants, especially those that usually serve locals, at around noon time and having to wait for long periods of time because the food is being prepared. A lot of tourists think that this is something to do with the general tardiness of Mexicans, but in reality, the tourists are forced to wait because they don't understand Mexican mealtimes. Mexican's don't eat at the same time you do back at home, which can be a bit surprising when you are new to the country. Below are the meals and mealtimes in Mexico.

The first meal in Mexico, eaten first thing in the morning, is a light breakfast that is referred to as *desayuno.* Desayuno usually consists of a beverage like hot chocolate, coffee, or a thick hot drink known as *atole,* accompanied by a fruit or sweet bread. Mexicans will eat a heavier breakfast or brunch known as *almuerzo* between 9 in the morning and noon. The *almuerzo* may consist of meat and egg dishes, *enchiladas,* tortillas, and *chilaquiles.*

The main meal of the day is referred to as *la comida* and is usually eaten between 2 and 4 pm. This explains why most restaurants that serve locals won't have food ready by noon. *La comida* typically consist of four courses, including salads, soups, the main dish, and dessert. Mexicans will wash down their *la comida* with a fruit flavored juice known as *agua fresca*. Some Mexicans may choose to wash down their *la comida* with an alcoholic beverage, such as a cocktail or beer.

The last meal of the day for many Mexicans usually eaten between 7 and 9 in the evening, is referred to as *la cena*. However, sometimes it can be eaten even later, depending on one's activities. In most cases, *la cena* consists of a hot beverage and bread, though you can eat a proper meal or some street-side tacos in its place. Over the course of the day, Mexicans will also eat plenty of snacks, such as *botanas, tostadas,* and *antojitos.*

Mexican Street Food

You will notice that in Mexico, food is not only served in cafes and restaurants. You will find several street-side food vendors, especially in the evenings, selling street foods such as tamales, quesadillas, tacos, churros, chalupas, and so on. Some foods sold on the street-side food stalls are informal, and you are therefore unlikely to eat them in a home or restaurant, but they are still amazingly delicious. They are also incredibly cheap, and it is possible to eat for your fullness while spending only a couple of dollars. Aside from the roadside food stalls, you will also find some very authentic Mexican dishes in the local markets.

The Metric System

Unlike countries like the United States, which use the Imperial System of weights and measurement, Mexico uses the metric system. Therefore, you will find that lengths and distances are measured in centimeters, meters, and kilometers, rather than inches, feet, yards, and miles. Weight is measured in grams and kilograms, rather than ounces and pounds. The volume of fluids is measured in milliliters and liters, rather than pints and gallons. Temperature is measured in degrees Celsius rather than degrees Fahrenheit. If you are used to the imperial system of measurement, all this can be very confusing. However, once you get used to it, you will notice that it is quite easy and straightforward.

To make it easier for you to understand the metric system, below are some common metric measurements and their equivalent measurement in the imperial system. Kindly note that the conversions with the ≈ symbol are approximate, rather than exact.

- 5 centimeters ≈ 2 inches
- 1 meter ≈ 39 inches
- 1 kilometer ≈ 0.6 miles
- 60 kph = 37 mph
- 90 kph = 56 mph
- 110 kph = 68 mph
- 1 kilogram ≈ 2.2 pounds
- 5 ml = 1 teaspoon
- 15 ml = 1 tablespoon
- 4 liters ≈ 1 gallon
- 27° Celsius = 80° Fahrenheit

The best way to get used to the different system of weights and measurements is to install a conversion app on your smartphone. This way, whenever you are in doubt, you can quickly convert and gain a better understanding of the measurements.

Mexican Traditions And Holidays

Many foreigners moving to Mexico also find themselves confused by Mexico's many holidays, especially the cultural ones that are rooted in ancient traditions and symbolism. Most of their traditional holidays are marked with lots of dance and celebrations, and even the holidays that are celebrated globally, are marked differently in Mexico. For instance, whereas children from all over the world wake up to Christmas gifts only on December 25th, children in Mexico also receive presents on the Three Kings Day, which is celebrated on January 6th. Below, let's take a look at some religious and public holidays observed in Mexico.

The Day Of The Dead

Also referred to as Hanal Pixan in Mayan and *Dia De Los Muertos* in Spanish, this is a holiday that is meant to celebrate the unity between life and death. The holiday seeks to remind people that death is part of the cycle of life. This celebration brings together ancient Aztec festivals and Catholic celebrations (Mexico is predominantly Catholic, though other religions are welcome in Mexico). The celebrations for the Day of the Dead commence on October 31st and continue in conjunction with the Catholic festivals of All Saints Day on the 1st of November and All Souls Day of the 2nd of November.

The Day of the Dead is a time of showing respect to departed loved ones. It is believed that during this time, the souls of the deceased come to celebrate with the living family members. People clean the altars of the deceased and leave gifts at the grave. They also put up altars for the dead at home and put up photographs of the deceased, as well as the things they loved – food, chocolates, alcoholic drinks, toys in case the deceased is a child, and other such items.

Las Posadas

This is the holiday that marks the beginning of Christmas festivities. This celebration, which starts on December 16th, takes place over 9 days of consecutive candlelight processions as families come together to re-enact the period Joseph and Mary spent looking for lodging in Bethlehem.

Noche Buena

This is where the Christmas festivities hit their crescendo. Noche Buena is celebrated on 24th December, is marked by attending mass at midnight, after which the families go back home to have Christmas supper. People open the gifts they received over the festivities and continue with the celebrations till late. Owing to the celebrations of Noche Buena, the 25th of December is treated as a day of rest in Mexico, as families feast on the leftovers from the celebrations from the previous day.

New Year's Day

Referred to as *Año Nuevo* in Mexico, New Year's Day in Mexico is celebrated on the first of January, just like in most other countries around the world. This is usually a time to celebrate with family and relax following the celebrations of ushering in the New Year.

The Three Kings Day

Also referred to as *Dia de Reyes* or *Día de los reyes magos* in Spanish, this is a celebration that commemorates the three Wise men arriving in Bethlehem bearing gifts for baby Jesus. The Three Kings Day is celebrated on January 6th, which is the day Mexican children wake up to find surprise gifts and toys. During *Dia de Reyes*, special bread is prepared with tiny plastic babies hidden inside the bread. Whoever gets a slice of bread containing one of the plastic babies is supposed to hold a party before or on the 2nd of February, which is the day that marks the end of the Christmas festivities.

Constitution Day

Referred to as *Dia de la Constitución* in Mexico, this is a public holiday that marks the day following the Mexican Revolution when the Mexican Constitution became official law. Constitution Day is marked on the first Monday of February.

Carnaval

This is a Mexican holiday that is based on Catholic festivities. The Carnaval, which takes place in late February or early March, kick-starts a celebration that lasts five days, during which people indulge in all the carnal pleasures they will be obligated to forego during the 40 days of Lent. Carnaval is a huge and spectacular festival, during which people dance and parade in the streets dressed in costumes. The most vibrant Carnival celebrations take place in Veracruz and La Paz. People do away with all their inhibitions and engage in drinking, dancing, and debauchery for the five days. People sometimes wear masks as a way of protecting themselves against evil spirits, though this is also a convenient way of engaging fully in the celebrations while remaining anonymous.

Semana Santa

Also referred to as Holy Week, this is a very important holiday season in Mexico, second only to the Christmas season. This holiday is meant to celebrate Easter and is celebrated between Palm Sunday and Easter Sunday. Since it is a whole week of festivities, many locals use this as a time to go on a small vacation. The crucifixion of Christ is also enacted in many small towns.

The Fifth Of May

A lot of foreigners wrongly assume that this holiday, which is also known as *Cinco de Mayo,* is Mexico's Independence Day. However, this holiday commemorates The Battle of Puebla in 1862, when the Mexicans defeated the French army. This holiday is mainly celebrated within the Mexican state of Puebla.

Independence Day

Locally known as *Dia de la Independencia,* this is the Day that marks the start of Mexico's fight for independence from the Spaniards. This holiday is marked on September 16. During this celebration, Mexicans from all across the country gather at midnight at the town square within their specific towns to make the independence shout "Viva Mexico" which was originally made on December 16, 1810, by Miguel Hidalgo. The celebrations also involve parades, dance and fireworks, and bullfights in some cities.

Other popular holidays in Mexico include Benito Juarez Day, celebrated on March 21th every year, Labor Day, which is celebrated on the first of May together with the rest of the world, Revolution Day, marked on November 20th.

Chapter Thirteen: Common Misconceptions About Mexico

As a country, Mexico is greatly misunderstood. Sensationalist news reporters and movies greatly misrepresent the country, and as a result, many foreigners, save for those who have actually been into the country, don't know much truth about Mexico. In the minds of a lot of foreigners, Mexico is either a cactus-filled desert, a beach resort destination, a corrupt and war-torn country under the mercies of cartels and drug lords, or a poor country whose every citizen is trying to move to the United States. However, all these are misconceptions and misrepresentations of Mexico. In this chapter, we are going to look at some common misconceptions about Mexico.

Mexico Is Dangerous

This is perhaps the most common and the most enduring misconceptions about Mexico. A lot of people who have never been to Mexico believe that the country is a very dangerous place, with runaway crime and a corrupt government that works according to the whims of the narco cartels. Like we saw, however, this is just a bogus claim.

While the narco cartels are there, they only operate in some parts of 5 states, out of the 31 states that make up the United Mexican States. This means that the majority of the country is fairly safe, while some parts are even safer than some of the US states. In addition, the Mexican government does not work according to the wishes of the cartels. Actually, the government has put up a very spirit fight in an attempt to rid Mexico of the drug cartels. Finally, the crime that is experienced in cities like Mexico City is the petty crime you will find in other big cities. Therefore, the claims that Mexico is a dangerous place are just that–baseless claims.

Mexico Is A Poor Country

During his campaign, US President complained so much about Mexican immigrants coming into the United States, that one of his major campaign promises was to build a wall that would stop Mexicans from moving to the US. This has led to the perception that everyone in Mexico is poor and is trying to cross into the US to work low-wage jobs. Most Americans perception of Mexicans is limited to what they have heard from the news and the Mexican immigrants they have met in America. Unfortunately, most of the Mexicans immigrating to Mexico are poor, so Americans who have seen no other Mexicans assume that this is a representation of every Mexican.

However, Mexico is not a poor country. While there are some poor Mexicans, not everyone is poor. In 2018, the IMF ranked Mexico as the 15th largest economy in the world. In terms of GDP, Mexico ranks at number 59. A number of Mexican households have a disposable income, and about half of the people in Mexico have a car. There is a growing middle class in the country, and the number of Mexicans pursuing higher education has more than tripled in the last three decades. Most of Mexico is developed and has most of the amenities you would expect to find in any other country. All this shows that Mexico is not the poor country many people take it to be.

Mexico Is In South America

Ask random people in your home country where Mexico is located, and the majority will tell you that it is in South America. Another significant portion of them will say that it is in Central America. Only a few of them will get it right–that Mexico is in North

America. Surprising, right? The misconception that Mexico is in south/central America comes from two things. First, most people think of North America as the United States. Funny enough, some people don't even think that of Canada as being part of North America. Therefore, they do not fathom Mexico as being part of North America. Second, Mexico is part of Latin America. Latin America refers to countries in the Americas where the main languages are either Spanish, French or Portuguese. Considering that the majority of countries in South America are part of Latin America, it is assumed that since Mexico is a part of Latin America, it is also a part of South America. Like I said, however, Mexico is completely a part of North America.

Mexico Is A Drug-Infested Country

With the drug cartels and the representation of Mexico as a drug capital in movies, most foreigners believe that Mexico is ridden with drugs. How wrong they are. Mexico is not a drug capital. Instead, it is just a conduit for drugs from Colombia and Peru into the United States. Mexico only got entangled into the drug trade because it shares a border with the United States. Mexicans themselves are very conservative, and drug use in the country is very rare. Generally, Mexicans view drugs as something for the gringos, and therefore, you will find some pushers selling coke and weed in the street corners of the touristy areas of Mexico. However, Mexicans themselves are not major drug users. Actually, if you come from countries like the United States, Canada or some European countries, your home country probably has a higher rate of drug use than Mexico.

Mexican Street Food Will Make You Sick

A lot of foreigners do not get to enjoy the delicacies of Mexican street food because they are afraid that this food will make them sick. They think that the ingredients of street food has been washed with tap water or haven't even been washed. However, you are actually more likely to get sick from dining at a fancy restaurant rather than a street-side food stall. This is because fancy restaurants might thaw and refreeze their meats and fish several times in case they are unable to sell all of it in a day. On the street, on the other hand, the food is fresh, bought that morning from the market, and all the food will be sold by the time the stall closes. Therefore, with street food, you are sure that you are consuming fresh food. I'll only give one tip when it comes to street food. Go for the stalls with a huge crowd of buyers or a long line of locals waiting to get served. The popular stalls are popular for a reason–the locals know they are clean and they serve the tastiest food.

Buses And Fowl

This is one of the most hilarious misconceptions I have heard about Mexico. If you ever watched the popular TV show *Prison Break*, there is a scene where one of the Characters, a Mexican, is heading home after breaking out of prison. Once he crosses the border, he gets onto a bus that is full of passengers carrying vegetables, fruits, and even live chicken on their laps. This is what many foreigners think about Mexico. They think that if you ride on a bus in Mexico, you will inevitably sit next to a passenger carrying a clucking, wing-flapping fowl, making for a very uncomfortable journey. However, this is just what the movies show. Once you get to Mexico, you will probably never encounter someone traveling with their chicken inside a bus for the entire duration of your stay in the country.

These above are just some of the most common misconceptions about our beloved country of Mexico. Of course, there are many other myths and misconceptions about Mexico, and like the above, many of them are just baseless. To avoid ending up believing such myths, next time someone tries to tell you something about Mexico, ask them if they have been to the country. If they haven't, they are probably feeding you hogwash.

Chapter Fourteen: Some Resources To Help You After Your Move To Mexico

After moving to a new country, it is obviously going to take you some time before you fully adapt to life in the new country. To make it easier for you to settle and adapt to life in Mexico, below are some resources that might come in handy.

Local News In English

After you settle down in your new city in Mexico, you might want to keep yourself aware of what is happening locally. However, most newspapers are written in Spanish, and reading the news can be challenging if you don't know the language. Fortunately, there are some publications that have English versions of their e-newspapers. Some of these include The News (local and international news and sports), Playa Maya News (community news for those around the Riviera Maya), Atencion San Miguel (news, community and culture in the San Miguel de Allende area), Mexico News Daily (local news, op-eds and sports), the Yucatan Times (local and international news) and the Mazatlán Post (news about Mazatlán and the rest of the country). Even some of the biggest newspapers, such as El Universal and El Sol de Mexico have an English news section.

Facebook Groups

The world's largest social media network is not only good for helping you keep in touch with your friends from back in high school, but it is also a great way of making friends in a new country and learning a thing or two about adapting to life in a new country. There is a high number of expats in Mexico, and there are several Facebook groups for expats, some focused on the entire country and some with a more local focus. Some Facebook groups for expats worth checking out include:

- Expats In Mexico
- Expats Living In Mexico
- US Expats Living In Mexico
- Yucatan Expat Life
- Merida Mexico Expat Community

Expat Groups And Societies

Aside from the online groups and communities, many expat areas also have groups and societies where the members meet in person and run various programs and activities. Such groups are a great way to meet new friends, learn various things that affect your life in Mexico, connect with people who are familiar with your language and culture, and get recommendations for trustworthy reliable workers (babysitters, plumbers, electricians, and so on). Some popular expats groups and societies in Mexico include:

- Canadian Club Of Lake Chapala – focused on Canadian expats within the Lake Chapala area
- Circle of Friends – focused on expats in the Torreon area.
- English Speakers in Action in Hermosillo – focused on English speaking expats and locals in Hermosillo in Sonora.
- The International Women's Club of Merida – focused on English speaking women within the Merida area.
- Lake Chapala Society – one of the most active societies with lots of members. Focused on expats in the Lake Chapala area.

While these are some of the most popular groups and societies, you can find similar societies within your city/town by just asking around within the community.

Important Numbers

When you have just moved to a new country, it is advisable to have some emergency contact information in case you find yourself in an emergency. Below are some numbers you should keep close at all times:

Police:	060
Emergency:	911
Red Cross:	065
Green Angels: for tourists)	078 (Roadside assistance
The US Embassy:	+55 5080 2000
Canadian Embassy:	01-800-706-2900
British Embassy:	+52 55 1670 3200

Final Words

Thank you for sticking with me to the end of the book.

That was quite a ride, but I hope that by now, you have learned all the important information you need to know before making your move to Mexico, and I hope you are excited about living in Mexico. Moving to Mexico will be a truly life-changing experience for you–a lower cost of living, a country that is teeming with culture and heritage, great weather, friendly and very helpful locals, lots of fun activities to engage in, an opportunity to practice your Spanish, amazing Mexican food, and so much more. What's more, the process of getting the right papers to settle in Mexico is pretty straightforward. There is nothing not to love about making the move to Mexico. It is no surprise that a high number of those who come to Mexico for a short time end up making the decision to settle in the country permanently.

Finally, before you go, I want to request you to take a minute to leave your honest review of the book. Your feedback is highly appreciated and helps me keep producing such great books for my readers.

Welcome to the land of tequila and Mariachi!

Made in the USA
Las Vegas, NV
02 October 2024

96109423R00080